Planning Your Postgraduate Research

Please return / renew by date shown.
You can renew at: **norlink.norfolk.gov.uk**
or by telephone: **0344 800 8006**
Please have your library card & PIN ready.

D1610815

Palgrave Study Skills

Business Degree Success
Career Skills
Cite Them Right (9th edn)
Critical Thinking Skills (2nd edn)
e-Learning Skills (2nd edn)
The Exam Skills Handbook (2nd edn)
The Graduate Career Guidebook
Great Ways to Learn Anatomy and
    Physiology
How to Begin Studying English Literature
    (3rd edn)
How to Manage Your Distance and Open
    Learning Course
How to Manage Your Postgraduate Course
How to Study Foreign Languages
How to Study Linguistics (2nd edn)
How to Use Your Reading in Your Essays
    (2nd edn)
How to Write Better Essays (3rd edn)
How to Write Your Undergraduate
    Dissertation
Improve Your Grammar
Information Skills
The International Student Handbook
IT Skills for Successful Study
The Mature Student's Guide to Writing
    (3rd edn)
The Mature Student's Handbook
The Palgrave Student Planner
Practical Criticism

Presentation Skills for Students (2nd edn)
The Principles of Writing in Psychology
Professional Writing (2nd edn)
Researching Online
Skills for Success (2nd edn)
The Student's Guide to Writing (3rd edn)
The Student Phrase Book
Study Skills Connected
Study Skills for International Postgraduates
Study Skills for Speakers of English as a
    Second Language
The Study Skills Handbook (4th edn)
Studying History (3rd edn)
Studying Law (3rd edn)
Studying Modern Drama (2nd edn)
Studying Psychology (2nd edn)
Teaching Study Skills and Supporting
    Learning
The Undergraduate Research Handbook
The Work-Based Learning Student
    Handbook
Work Placements – A Survival Guide for
    Students
Write it Right (2nd edn)
Writing for Engineers (3rd edn)
Writing for Law
Writing for Nursing and Midwifery Students
    (2nd edn)
You2Uni

Pocket Study Skills

14 Days to Exam Success
Blogs, Wikis, Podcasts and More
Brilliant Writing Tips for Students
Completing Your PhD
Doing Research
Getting Critical
Planning your dissertation
Planning Your Essay
Planning Your PhD

Reading and Making Notes
Referencing and Understanding Plagiarism
Reflective Writing
Report Writing
Science Study Skills
Studying with Dyslexia
Success in Groupwork
Time Management
Writing for University

Palgrave Research Skills

Authoring a PhD
The Foundations of Research (2nd edn)
Getting to Grips with Doctoral Research
Getting Published
The Good Supervisor (2nd edn)

The Postgraduate Research Handbook (2nd
    edn)
The Professional Doctorate
Structuring Your Research Thesis

For a complete listing of all our titles in this area please visit
www.palgrave.com/studyskills

Planning Your Postgraduate Research

Margaret Walshaw

 macmillan
education   palgrave

First published 2015 by
PALGRAVE

Palgrave in the UK is an imprint of Macmillan Publishers Limited,
registered in England, company number 785998, of 4 Crinan Street,
London N1 9XW.

Palgrave Macmillan in the US is a division of St Martin's Press LLC,
175 Fifth Avenue, New York, NY 10010.

Palgrave is a global academic imprint of the above companies
and is represented throughout the world.

Palgrave® and Macmillan® are registered trademarks in the United States,
the United Kingdom, Europe and other countries

ISBN: 978-1-137-42734-2

This book is printed on paper suitable for recycling and made from fully
managed and sustained forest sources. Logging, pulping and manufacturing
processes are expected to conform to the environmental regulations of the
country of origin.

A catalogue record for this book is available from the British Library.

A catalog record for this book is available from the Library of Congress.

Printed in China

Contents

List of Case Studies

List of Activities

Acknowledgements

This book was written for postgraduate researchers. My greatest debt is to my own postgraduate researchers for sharing with me their hopes, joys, confusions and frustrations along the research journey. I am indebted to them for insights into their own experiences and for allowing me to quote them in the examples.

I am grateful to the many supervisors and colleagues with whom I have been privileged to co-supervise. Their knowledge, expertise and sound common sense has deepened my own understanding of what the research experience might mean for postgraduate researchers.

I also thank Palgrave for support and encouragement in writing the book. Della Oliver, Helen Caunce and Ann Edmondson all provided helpful assistance and much appreciated advice. It has been a pleasure to work with them and their team at Palgrave.

Preface

Welcome to *Planning Your Postgraduate Research*. The book is designed to improve your skills and practical knowledge about research during the early stages of the process. It is principally aimed at those who are undertaking extended pieces of research. The book is not intended to replace the knowledge that classic books on research offer. Rather, the intention is to supplement that knowledge by allowing you to develop a skills set that will provide critical starting points for undertaking research. It focuses on research at a practical level, providing you with skills and understandings about how to get started and progress to the proposal stage without being overwhelmed with unfamiliar language, complex ideas and self-doubt. By exposing you to essential learning and research skills you will begin to grow in confidence and look positively towards the prospect of undertaking research.

There is a lot more to research than making important discoveries. Often what seems natural and commonsense to experienced researchers might seem mysterious to the novice postgraduate researcher. Research demands specific skills and practical knowledge. Once you have developed those craft skills you will be well on the way to completing a successful thesis or dissertation. The kinds of skills and practical knowledge you need are wide-ranging. For example, you need to know what a literature review is, why you need one, and what you need to do to write a good one. You need to know what kind of information about your chosen topic will be valued within the research community, where and how to find that information and how to record it. You also need to know what a research proposal looks like and why you need to produce one. Research is embedded within a host of requirements and conventions. If you are not aware of these you are likely to underestimate or overestimate what is required.

This down-to-earth book is designed to improve your skills and understandings about research. It will help sharpen your thinking, enhance your skills and capture the underlying structures and principles necessary for bringing critical inquiry to bear on your research interest. Whether you are embarking on a 100,000 word thesis or something considerably smaller, such as a research report, you will need to work your way through the planning cycle in order to acquire the approval to undertake your research. My experience confirms that postgraduate researchers often lack a clear understanding of what kinds of skills and knowledge are required for undertaking research. This book fills in the gaps left open by others – by books and by people – and lets you in on the secrets of research skill development. Each chapter explores a unique aspect of research preparation. From finding out what research is all about through to the development of your own research proposal – and all the stages in between – this book traces the significant milestones on your journey and sets out to make the intangible aspects of those milestones real.

Overlaying each of the chapters is a tacit recognition of the importance of attending to your own health and well-being. Taking care of your mental, emotional and spiritual well-being will become tremendously important in sustaining your interest throughout the project. Research is never plain sailing. It is an activity that provides scope for the full range of human emotions. No matter how much careful planning is undertaken, there are likely to be ups and downs. One way to keep level-headed is to schedule in time to enjoy your favourite activities and relaxations, such as jogging or watching movies. Be sure to set aside a realistic amount of time for family and for the friends who are supportive of what you are doing. If you look after your well-being then you will have the personal resources to deal with moments of self-doubt when things go wrong. You will also have an inner strength to deal with the feedback you will receive as your project moves forward into the discovery stage. By fine tuning your personal as well as your practical research tool-kit, you will make the most important discovery of all – that you possess the necessary practical knowledge to negotiate your way successfully through the early stages of the research maze.

The book provides a comprehensive but integrated introduction to research development from the early planning stages through to the successful research proposal. Each chapter begins with an overview of the key concepts or themes discussed in that chapter. Ideas and key concepts are developed at a level that is accessible to someone who has little or no familiarity with the material discussed. At the end of each chapter you will find a summary of the main points and key terms covered. Towards the end of the book a glossary of key terms is provided for your easy reference.

The book is intended to be used interactively. The activities within each chapter are provided as opportunities for you to enhance your knowledge and understanding more acutely. By asking you to examine your own understanding and to reflect on particular points emphasized in each chapter, the activities allow you to make stronger connections between the book's content and your own experiences and unique situation. They will help you steer a straight course through the process and navigate your way out of the difficulties and dilemmas that are typically encountered. Case study stories embedded within the text recount the personal experiences of either my own postgraduate researchers or those of fictitious characters that I have created. Together with insights from postgraduate researchers provided throughout the book, the case studies serve to contextualize the material and provide emphasis on important points.

Overview of chapters

The volume consists of seven chapters:

1   Introducing research
2   Making early decisions
3   Gathering and evaluating relevant literature
4   Writing the literature review
5   Defining a research methodology
6   Creating a research proposal
7   Looking ahead to the next steps

Chapter 1 looks at the bigger picture of what research is about, particularly within the social sciences and humanities. It explores the multi-pronged larger view of research, allowing you to understand where your own project might sit within the larger scheme. Each view of research has its own purposes, yet each allows the researcher to address questions of specific interest. In setting out the purposes of research, the chapter draws attention to the numerous and sometimes conflicting reasons that drive different researchers in their work. It showcases these differences by providing practical examples. Rather than focusing on the challenges and demands involved in research activity, Chapter 1 points to the positive aspects of participating in a research programme, offering baseline information to clarify what the researcher is required to know in order to undertake research at this level.

Appreciating what research is about involves an understanding of the stages in the process. Chapter 1 maps out a sequence for advancing from preliminary ideas to the completion of a research proposal. In doing that, it emphasizes the point that, whilst the sequence is imminently progressive, it is not always linear. Rather, it is often circular or iterative. Conducting research is a privilege, but it also carries certain responsibilities. One of those responsibilities lies in understanding the process and core research concepts. Another responsibility is to ensure that the planned research will be ethically informed. Ethical decision-making is focused on standards and norms that produce the best outcomes for the participants in your research, and the chapter outlines best practice to meet those standards. There are many informants who will be able to offer guidance on your research journey. The key is to optimize the support that is conducive to responsible and best practice.

Chapter 2 puts your preliminary ideas under scrutiny and guides you towards formulating them in a way that is consistent with conventional research practice. This is the real beginnings of your research – where you firm up on what you going to do and work at developing the shape that your project will take. The starting point for every project lies in a good idea. The idea should not only seem 'good' to you but there should be an expectation that it will be considered worthwhile by the research community. Experienced researchers shape their good idea into a topic worthy of investigation and then proceed to explore a specific aspect of the topic through a research question. The thing to be aware of is that the topic you choose and the research question you formulate will guide everything you do in your research activity. For this reason, it is important that you are truly interested in or even passionate about your chosen subject, and that you do not rush when making your topic decision.

Emerging researchers generally have wonderfully good ideas. Postgraduate researchers are no exception. Whatever the objective, invariably the idea will need to be condensed in size, trimmed back to make it manageable and researchable to suit the time and resources you have available. In this chapter you learn how to establish boundaries around your topic to ensure it is clearly contained and well defined. You learn what counts as a good research question. You also learn what kinds of questions will not be useful in the research process and what questions will not allow you to find answers to what you are interested in. The importance of defining the concepts you plan to use is emphasized. You will explore how a conceptual framework provides a map of the relationships between those ideas, and how it illustrates the coherence of, and provides justification for, your research.

Chapter 3 provides you with the skills to become familiar with the literature in your chosen area of study. Most postgraduate researchers find reading the literature a most rewarding experience. Reading the literature will help you clarify what has already been found or achieved in your area of study. In many ways effective reading of the literature assists you in determining whether or not your chosen topic, as defined by your research question, is likely to be of interest to the research community and whether or not it will lead to a significant piece of research. By reading the literature you will fairly quickly come to an appreciation of whether or not your proposed study will contribute to new knowledge.

In this chapter you will explore the different types of literature available and learn what sources of information are valued within the research community. You will learn about print and on-line material and citation indices, as well as the difference between primary and secondary sources. We look at how to select search terms in order to conduct a library literature search and you will learn the importance of saving your sources and organizing them in a reference database. Widening your search to include institutional or national reports and policies, as well as archival material, media reports and information from informal channels, may well be important to your search. In this chapter you will discover that simply accessing sources is not sufficient – you need to evaluate each the literature sources you find to determine its merit and relevance to your own proposed work.

Chapter 4 takes you through the processes involved in writing a literature review. The importance of the literature review cannot be overstated. It will help you situate your own study within the context of the existing body of knowledge relating to your chosen topic area. Not only that, later on your review will inform your discussion of the findings from your data. You will use the literature that you review to compare and contrast your own findings, and you will draw on it to establish the particular contribution your project has made to the field. The job of accessing, reading, screening and evaluating the available literature in your chosen area does not stop once you have completed your first draft of your literature review. It is a task that continues throughout the research project.

From your wide reading on the subject area you will have begun to assemble a considerable number of papers, reports, and other documents relevant to your topic and specific research question. In this chapter we consider how to organize the material in a way that will lead to a structured and logically prepared review. You will learn about the process of synthesizing your sources and how to make decisions about what to include and what to exclude. You will discover in your reading that terms and expressions are often used differently from one author to another. If defining terms is important, so is consistent referencing. You wil need to construct your own position on the topic. Once established, this position is maintained throughout the review. It will allow you to construct a coherent argument for undertaking the research you plan.

Chapter 5 explores what we mean by methodology and research methods and introduces you to research designs and approaches for gathering and analyzing data. Decisions surrounding your design choice are important because they will influence the kinds and level of findings you make. They will also impact on the conclusions that you are able to draw. Your choice of research design will align with the purpose of your research. You might be focused on finding a solution to a problem or a puzzle, or you might be focused on investigating differences over time or in initiating change within a setting. Alternatively, you might lean towards developing a new understanding or a new explanation. Your research design will suit your main objectives for your research. Good research designs are fit for purpose.

In this chapter you are working towards the development of a coherent approach to undertaking your research. You need to demonstrate clear links between the key objectives of your research and your proposed data collection and analysis. Your research question is central to establishing those links. The research question will guide your decisions over the kind of data that need to be collected. It will indicate where you might find the source of the data you need for your project and, possibly, when you might collect it. The methods you choose to collect your data and the tools that you use to access the dataset will depend on what you want to find out and how you want to find it out. In this chapter we explore alternative approaches that will guide you towards firming up these important decisions in your own project.

Chapter 6 moves us towards the endpoint of the early stages of thesis work. This is the chapter in which we discuss the research proposal: its purpose as well as the content that you will need to include. By now you will have given considerable thought to the question of how your research will contribute to the academic discussion and debate within your chosen area. You will have identified all the steps you need to take in order to conduct your research. The research proposal puts all this information together in a way that maps out a rationale for your research and spells out the precise way in which your research will be undertaken. While you will be asked to produce a research proposal for your planned research as part of the requirements for your qualification, the research proposal is not simply a requirement for postgraduate researchers. It is a central feature of the work that all researchers do before they conduct their research.

In research, the successful proposal provides a formal reassurance to supervisors and others that you know exactly what is going to be investigated, why the study needs to be undertaken and how it will be done, and that you have the capacity and resources to successfully complete the investigation in the timeframe provided. In this chapter we will identify the specific components that the panel assessing your proposal will be looking for and will demonstrate how that can be achieved. You are likely to be asked to speak about and defend your proposed research, so we look at the importance of articulating your thoughts clearly. A successful defence will enable you to proceed directly with the research. The chapter also takes you through the steps to consider when applying for ethical clearance.

Chapter 7 takes a wide-angled look at the next steps in the research process. Having completed the research proposal and being given the thumbs-up for your research the excitement of being in the field or immersed in archives or working with others will truly strike home. There is much to do and it is a time of high tension when things do not always go according to plan. Building a degree of flexibility into your plans will help accommodate changes in the context and setting of the study and will help you make adjustments when things go wrong. Coping with the highs and lows of the research process is part and parcel of the journey.

The most influential form of support you receive during your research will almost certainly be provided by your supervisor or advisor. The best supervision relationships are effective and productive for you, both to ensure that the research is completed on time, and, importantly, to ensure that you grow intellectually (Green and Usher, 2003; Kamler and Thomson, 2006). Examiners of your work will expect to read a logical and coherent argument presented with attention to grammar and free from typographical errors. Once successfully examined, getting your work 'out there' to a wider audience is the primary means by which you will be able to have an influence on the thinking within your discipline. Presentations to the academic, professional, practitioner and policy communities, to industry and commercial representatives and to the general public through the media, are all certain ways of getting your work disseminated. Presentations also give you the opportunity of forming long-term networks, associations and potential collaborations.

1 Introducing Research

The research process

Research is all around us. Barely a week goes by when we don't read or hear about studies that researchers are undertaking. We learn about medical and scientific breakthroughs. We read about worldwide as well as local solutions to contemporary concerns and issues, and we are informed of the results of opinion polls and market research. For example, we know from research that some kinds of 'thinking' activities delay the onset of Alzheimer's disease. We also know, as a result of scientific developments and medical research, that confirmation of paternity is much easier today than it was a few decades ago. Sometimes research is carried out when a person or organization is searching for a new approach. Sometimes the researcher is sceptical of the available knowledge; there may be conflicting evidence or no information available. Researchers who carry out all these types of work are undertaking an important role in contemporary life. The point to note is the way they go about making their discoveries; it is not haphazard and the discoveries are not brought about simply through flashes of inspiration (Gray, 2004). Researchers use highly structured processes to produce new knowledge (Carter, Kelly and Brailsford, 2012).

Albeit on a smaller scale, you will also be doing research in a disciplined way to find out something about the world in which we live. Whatever your research goal, when the time comes to carry out the research, you will be following a series of conventions. You might be interested in understanding something or some people, and in fathoming out what is going on. You might be focused on analyzing a puzzle and finding a solution. You might be more interested in theorizing and in explaining things in a new way. You might want to change and improve a situation. You might want to evaluate an intervention. Or you might want to explore differences in events over time or through precise experimentation. Irrespective of your research intention, once you enrol in a research course or programme you will need

1

to comply with the 'research way of knowing'. Academic research is an organized, systematic, logical and rigorous process of inquiry (Crotty, 1998; Denscombe, 2003).

Your research will demonstrate a disciplined approach to answering the questions that you pose. It will involve thinking, planning and organizing. It will take you to the literature on your topic. It will see you gathering and analyzing data. It will involve you in offering explanations of what you have discovered. It will see you putting forward an argument, threaded through the chapters and/or sections of the written work you produce at the end of the process. The research process will, if carefully carried out, guarantee that your findings will be taken seriously.

Research at the postgraduate level is a long and complex activity, becoming even more complex as you proceed along the academic path (Burton and Steane, 2005). It involves a lot of questioning and requires an element of risk-taking. You will either make the discoveries you expect or you won't. In fact, you might make a discovery that is different from the one you expected. Don't be concerned about this. If you follow the conventional process, your anticipated (and unanticipated) discoveries will contribute to new knowledge. The process is not necessarily always straightforward, of course. Research is never absolutely cut-and-dried. There are many decisions to make and there are often unexpected problems to solve along the way. Research can never provide a final answer, but good research can offer us the best available understanding and explanation of an aspect of our world at this moment in time.

INSIGHTS FROM A POSTGRADUATE RESEARCHER

"The research process taught me much. At times it was extremely difficult. At other times it was a source of great satisfaction. I regularly doubted my ability to complete the task, whether I had gathered any data at all, and if I did have data, would it mean anything? Irrespective of having been warned this could be the case when I first started the research, I believe you always feel that it will happen to someone else and not you. But these feelings are part and parcel of the research process."

Be assured that at this stage no-one expects you to be completely familiar with the process. After all, your enrolment in a research programme of study is considered a research apprenticeship (Felton, 2008). As an apprentice, with supervisors' guidance, you get to participate in new experiences over a sustained period of time, giving your attention to learning about something from a new perspective (Wisker, 2007). Unlike courses you have done previously, where the planning and focus of attention was already established for you, in a research programme of study you get to call the shots. You take control of the project, conceptualizing it, customizing its design, shaping its development and setting its boundaries. Like an artist with a blank canvas, you build up from solid and reliable foundational knowledge and, with the new insights developed in the process of your work, you produce a project that is unique to you. In taking the initiative you put your particular stamp on your project.

Of course your personal stamp must not stray from the conventions of research. You will need to demonstrate that you have mastered those conventions in the report that you produce at the end of your research course. Irrespective of whether the report consists of a thesis, a project report, a dissertation, published articles or a series of shorter papers, the requirement is for a carefully planned and systematic piece of inquiry. In particular, you will need to show that you are able to conceptualize and design the study and undertake the data collection and analysis. You will need to demonstrate a sound understanding of the literature and the wider context of knowledge within which the work is embedded. Moreover, you will need to provide evidence of a critical and scholarly argument that is communicated clearly and coherently. Through all these aspects you will become the quintessential independent learner and, in the process, your skills and development and competency as a researcher will be enhanced (Scott and Usher, 2003).

INSIGHTS FROM A POSTGRADUATE RESEARCHER

"My research was indeed a voyage of discovery and the benefits of study are huge. Your brain starts working again and you become more passionate about learning and about your topic area."

What makes academic research distinctive

Much of the research we engage with in everyday life is focused on finding out facts. For example, researchers wanting to know how often women in their 20s use mobile phones would gather data on relevant aspects of phone usage. Along the way, they might find out some interesting facts. However, the research cannot explain to them why young women use mobile phones in the way they do. The research can describe the data but it cannot offer explanations of the data. Research data, by themselves, are simply facts. Theses, dissertations or small research projects must do something more than describe, which is a rather modest objective. They must, instead, analyze, explain, consider in the light of prior theory, test hypotheses, draw conclusions, generalize to other situations, explore limits to such generalizations, or contribute to theory development (Bernath and Vidal, 2007).

Within academic research it is possible to make sense of what might be happening in the data. We can test a hunch as well as build explanations of the data. From those explanations it is possible to predict and plan for the future. Academic research does this by connecting the data to a theory. Theories allow researchers to develop a set of propositions that explain *why* things happen as they do. For example, a researcher interested in staff dynamics might want to know why some employees in one department of a workplace demonstrate a greater commitment to their work than do employees from another department in the same workplace. A theory involving the category of 'communities of practice' might be invoked to frame the study (Lantolf, 2004). Relevant concepts and their interrelationships from the chosen theory will be used to organize and analyze the data and, as a result, the researcher will be able to draw a number of conclusions about employees' commitment to their work.

Perhaps, an academic researcher is interested in why children from some ethnic minority groups achieve significantly higher in cognitive tasks than children from other ethnic minority groups in the same school. The researcher might speculate that home practices, expectations, values and norms play a critical role in a child's cognitive development. The researcher will collect appropriate and relevant data from the home setting to enable the chosen factors to be explored. From the analysis the researcher will be able to test the theory initially proposed. When the theory is found to offer a credible explanation of differential cognitive achievement then the research makes a contribution to our understanding and, in this case, may become an important informer of policy and social planning.

In academic research, data and theory are truly interdependent (Bernath and Vidal, 2007). Whether the theory or the data come first in the process, their interdependence allows both data and theory to become meaningful and offer explanatory power. By themselves, neither theory nor data are particularly useful to research. Research that provides a theory but no data is speculation. In the research relating to cognitive difference amongst minority groups, unless the researcher is able to support the theory with a dataset, then the theory would simply be a guess or a hunch. That is not to ignore the fact that the theory might undergo some refinement during the research process. However, it does emphasize the interdependence of data and theory in academic research.

Similarly, research that provides data without theory simply reports on data collection. In the workplace example, the researcher might gather interesting data on the numbers and kinds of employees committed to their work, but unless the data are theorized, the researcher is not in a position to explain the employees' commitment to work. The report produced is likely to read more like a technical report than a contribution to the literature.

The technical report may well expertly describe the workplace environment but unless it explains the data it will leave little mark on business studies literature. In academic research the goal is to go beyond mere description. Academic researchers aim for careful analyses to enable them to explain what they have found in their research. The activity of linking a dataset and a theory together is how academic research achieves that goal.

Core research concepts

Anyone embarking on a new activity is introduced to new terminology. Take, for instance, children learning to play rugby at school. Initially the coach will talk in a language that seems unclear to the children but, as their experience with the sport grows, terms relevant to the game such as 'tackle', 'drop goal' and 'forward pass' will begin to take on the meaning that is shared by rugby players, supporters and officials. The same experience is likely to happen for new researchers. Experienced researchers have their own vocabulary. You may not have come across some of the terms before. Others, such as 'sample', might be familiar, but the research meaning might be new to you. And, as you might expect in a book for novice researchers, you will find a glossary of terms at the end of the book.

Activity

KEY RESEARCH TERMS
Consider the key research terms listed in the glossary at the end of the book.

1. Check the terms that are unfamiliar to you.
2. Start a file of your own glossary as you come across new terms in your reading.
3. Build up your glossary during the course of your research.

Steps involved in the early stages of research

Now that you have determined what practical steps you need to take to prepare successfully for the adventure ahead, it's time we looked at the academic requirements relating to the early stages of a research undertaking. Some of the steps might involve you in planning for primary research in which you directly explore your area of interest through methods such as observation, interviewing, and experimentation. Other steps might involve you in planning for secondary research in which you explore your area of interest through the literature, reports, archival records and so forth.

1. Planning and conceptualizing the research

Finding the topic

If you want to understand things better then you need to map out a well-defined, bounded topic that is both researchable and significant. The topic will need to be appropriate and manageable for your research course. For example, if you are an honours student then your topic will be much more contained than that of a doctoral student who is interested in the same area. More than likely, the course work you have already undertaken and your wider experiences will have pointed you towards an area that you would like to pursue. Even so, many postgraduate researchers find that firming up on the topic takes longer than expected. During the process of identifying the topic, postgraduate researchers typically want to investigate something that is too broad in scope, or involves participants to whom they are not likely to gain access, or involves resources (especially the resource of time) that are simply not available.

Developing research questions

The way of developing new knowledge within research is to pose questions and then attempt to answer them. The research questions you develop represent what you are trying to find out. Every research purpose requires a different kind of research question. What is going on? What is the solution? How can this be explained more clearly? How can this be improved? How effective is this? Each kind of question provides a focus and a guide for your research activity. Research can deal with questions that are open and exploratory since answers can be found, but it cannot deal with moral questions or questions relating to aesthetics. Good research questions reduce your area of interest to something more manageable and limited in scope. For these reasons, formulating good research questions is a key skill you need to develop.

Understanding the relevant literature

The focus of your work will not have emerged in a vacuum. Reading and thinking about the literature in relation to your topic are critical stages in the planning of your research. Coming to terms with the discussions and debates in your topic area will allow the focus of your study to emerge. Reading about findings from past research allows you to understand what has already been said and done in your chosen area of interest. Engaging with past work will enable you to make connections between your proposed focus and the existing debates in the field. In understanding the relevant literature you will become familiar with the figures of authority in the field, the landmark studies, the typical methodologies and theories, and where your topic fits into the broader picture.

Synthesizing the literature to create a need for your study

As you read more of the academic and professional literature you will begin to get a sense of the various conversations taking place. When you start to synthesize those conversations, a number of gaps and alternative approaches to doing things will open up in your thinking. The process allows you to see how you might fill a gap or offer another approach to the literature. Synthesizing the literature is a critical step for the development of a rationale for your study. The need for your study will become clear as you work out comparisons and contrasts between your proposed work and the work documented in the literature. Crucially, when you synthesize the literature with care, you will be able to see where you might be able to make a contribution.

2. Designing the research

Clarifying the research design

The design of your research establishes the practical plan for your study. It is systematic and logical and will be chosen to suit the purpose of your research. Different purposes require different kinds of research questions and these, in turn, initiate different research designs. When the fit between the purpose, the questions and design is good, your research will hold together well. The design will provide a coherent plan for undertaking the research. It will demonstrate a conceptual integrity between the purpose of your research and your decisions concerning the information and data needed, the ways in which you will collect and analyze the data (the research methods), the numbers and kinds of participants in your study, and how you will report the findings.

Specifying the data collection methods

The research design you choose will guide you towards a possible dataset for answering your research questions. Your data collection methods will depend on what you want to find out and who and where you want to find it out from. Context does matter. Quantitative methods are used to gather measurable data and qualitative methods are used to collect and explain descriptions of human behaviour. Survey (Rosier, 1988), interview (Gillham, 2000) and observation (Adler and Adler, 1994) are sometimes used, as are non-obtrusive data collection methods such as collecting from archival records, the internet, newspapers, magazines and artefacts. Data tools, which assist with the data collection, include questionnaires, focus groups, field notes, tests, observation checklists and records, interview schedules, written, audio and video recordings, journals and portfolios (Holly, 1997; Hurst, Wilson and Cramer, 1998; Jones, 2001; Ortlipp, 2008). When you are making data collection decisions, keep in mind the scale of the project and the material resources and time you have available.

Specifying the data analysis methods

When the dataset has been collected, you will need to sort, organize, process, code and analyze it. Electronic processing, such as spreadsheets and statistical software, makes this task easier. Just as data collection is a requirement of an empirical study, so too, is data analysis, principally because the analysis connects your data with your conclusions (Denzin and Lincoln, 2003; Willig, 2012). The decisions you make about how you will analyze your data will influence the decisions you make about what data you will collect – and not the other way around. Many postgraduate researchers overlook that important fact but, if you keep the point foremost in your mind, then you may feel less overwhelmed by the data. Applying systematic analytical methods will enable you to produce sound results and findings, and will help instil confidence in the conclusions you draw.

3. Preparing the research proposal

Outlining the background to the research

A research proposal provides a plan that outlines how you intend to conduct your research. In the proposal you identify what issue you intend to investigate, how you will go about addressing the issue, what we will learn from the study, and why you consider it is important to carry it out. In outlining the background you provide a context to the study, letting the reader know something about the topic, what has already been discovered about it, and why you are interested in pursuing it further. If your interest stems from purely personal reasons, you might want to locate yourself within the study by clarifying your personal background and knowledge in relation to the area of work. You then lead into a clear statement of the purpose of the study, explaining your overall aim and objectives and outlining the questions that will guide the research.

Clarifying the literature to create a need for the study

Proposals need a well-planned literature review which is usually reasonably extensive. The research proposal reports on what is known in your area by focusing on what has been done before. In the literature review you summarize published articles, records and documents, synthesize the literature base and offer a critique. The synthesis is intended to highlight major shortfalls or a 'gap' in the current knowledge base and offer a rationale for your proposed research. In the proposal you develop an argument or make a case for your intended research, establishing why you deem it necessary to conduct the proposed investigation and what your study will contribute to the research community.

Outlining the research methods

The methodology section discusses in detail how you will collect, analyze and present the data from the research. The choice of methods should be appropriate to the research questions. This section will clarify the research design. It will describe, in detail, the tools you will use to gather data, who will take part in the study (if appropriate), how you will select those people, when and where the research will be conducted, and how you will gain access to the site. It will discuss the methodological literature in relation to your research focus and the criteria you employed to make your methodological decisions. Your discussion will justify why your methods are feasible and appropriate as a means of answering your research question. It will also explain how you intend to organize and analyze the data collected.

Box 1.1 captures the early stages in research, showing the stages as following in orderly progression. Experienced researchers will be quick to point out that, although the depiction of sequential order is reasonably close, the stages do often overlap. For example, you might determine your topic early on, but the more you read of the literature the less convinced you are that the topic is precisely what you want to research.

Box 1.1 Typical early stages in research

1. Planning and conceptualizing the research
   - Finding a topic
   - Developing research questions
   - Understanding the relevant literature
   - Synthesizing the literature to demonstrate a need for the study
2. Designing the research
   - Clarifying the participants and location
   - Specifying the data collection methods
   - Specifying the data analysis methods
3. Preparing the research proposal
   - Outlining the background to the research
   - Clarifying the literature to demonstrate a need for the research
   - Outlining the research methods

Preparing yourself for research

Demonstrating independence and initiative is part of the job specification for anyone undertaking research. Your research programme is not likely to supply you with a detailed curriculum. At the postgraduate level, you will be the person who is ultimately held responsible for the work. Consider the enhanced responsibility over your own learning as a privilege. At what other times in your life as a learner in an educational institution have you had the opportunity to take so much control over your learning? How often before have you been encouraged to follow your own interests and passions? When has anyone previously given you licence to be creative and inventive? Chances are, the answer to all these questions is either 'not often' or 'never'.

There are certainly a number of positives about doing research. However, there are also a number of challenges.

INSIGHTS FROM A POSTGRADUATE RESEARCHER

"Undertaking research is not for the faint hearted. It requires focus, dedication, hard work and more time than is possible in any one day. It also requires a little bit of masochism as researchers tend to put themselves under more pressure than any sane person would. However, there are positive spin-offs, not the least of which is the feeling of success – and relief – you have when it all comes together and you finally reach that lofty summit."

There is certainly a lot of hard work ahead, and you need to prepare yourself for that, but you can begin by setting yourself up for the journey. Prepare your workspace. Perhaps more importantly, *clear* your workspace of irrelevant material. Check out how you are expected to present your work on paper – font, size, margins, line spacing and so forth – and set up templates on your computer accordingly. Be sure to date each document to avoid any confusion with your last update. If you prefer to read hard copies of publications, consider organizing the publications within a manila folder according to theme. Buy yourself any necessary stationery and think about purchasing a diary or journal to keep track of ideas and/or events. Keep a notebook beside your bed to jot down all those inspirations and solution pathways which will appear out of nowhere in the middle of the night.

Take advantage of any workshops your university offers to postgraduate researchers. Enjoy the intellectual stimulation your peers offer (Flores and Nerad, 2012). Some postgraduate researchers agree to meet informally at regular intervals over coffee or breakfast. If you are an international postgraduate researcher you may have access to support and friendship from a cohort of international postgraduate researchers (Ingleton and Cadman, 2002). In addition, consider setting up an arrangement for a critical friend (Costa and Kallick, 1993), someone who is willing to act as a sounding board for your ideas. Since friends can influence your chances of succeeding, stay clear of relationships that create ongoing tension for you. Avoid conflict situations and reap the benefits of the support you do receive, sometimes from unexpected sources. This support will keep you focused during the rough patches of your study.

> **INSIGHTS FROM A POSTGRADUATE RESEARCHER**
>
> *"Small steps, plenty of support people and a belief in yourself are the key factors that will help you scale these lofty heights. And the pay-off is huge."*

There will be challenges along the way. However, remember that you might perceive as a strength something that someone else perceives as a challenge or a weakness. For example, in relation to the requirement of independence, are you a leader or a follower? Do you like taking charge and working things out for yourself, or do you prefer to be told what to do? Are you organized and systematic? Weighing up your pluses with your minuses will be crucial to your personal and academic development. Ask yourself whether you readily accept information, or do you run a critical and sceptical eye over everything you read or hear? Are you undertaking this research with an inquiring and open mind or are you undertaking it to reinforce your own prejudices? An open mind, a disciplined approach, a proactive stance, and a critical assessment of what you read, are all useful dispositions that will help you navigate your way through the process successfully.

Then there are your current skills to consider. Are you at ease using computer technology? Do you know how to number pages and create an automatic table of contents? Are you familiar with back-up procedures for your work? You certainly do not want your work to end up lost in cyberspace. Do you have good library skills? What about your reading skills and your note-taking habits? How would you rate them both at this moment in time? Then there's the matter of your writing skills. Can you put together a clear and logical argument? More practical considerations also need to be addressed. What resources will you be able to access, in terms of printing and photocopying, seminars, conference attendance funding, workspace, and so forth, from your institution?

Your answers to these and similar questions will help you figure out what you know already (the positives) and what you need to know (the negatives). Once you identify the challenges you will be well placed to consider the practical steps you need to take to prepare yourself before you proceed further.

Activity

PREPARING MYSELF FOR RESEARCH
1. Set up a table with three columns, headed *Positives*, *Negative*, and *Action Plan for Negatives*. Enter as many rows as you need.
2. Alongside each negative entry, describe in the *Action Plan* column how you plan to address the problem.

Setting your timetable

Now that you have identified the strengths you bring to the work and noted what you might do to address any shortcomings, setting a timetable is a logical next step. Many postgraduate researchers overlook this important task – some with dire consequences. If there is unlikely to be any curriculum for your study, then you need to take control. Be proactive. Establish a pattern for your work so that you will be able to complete the preparation of the research proposal in a timely fashion. Of course, as a start, you will need to know when the research proposal is to be submitted. Find out the final date for the submission and factor in time for any unforeseen eventualities.

Ask yourself whether you prefer to work in bursts or whether you do best with steady application to the work. How will your preferences to work affect any timetable that you establish? What other commitments – such as those relating to work, home, family, study, or sport and hobbies – do you have that might prevent you from developing a regular pattern of study during the course of the work? Unless you stop to identify and build in time for these other commitments then the timetable you develop will not be of much use.

As an example, a doctoral student mapped out a timeline for her thesis and entered as much detail as she could for the early stages of her work, leading to the research proposal. While your research may not be for a doctoral qualification, no matter what level of research you are undertaking you will still need to commit to a clear completion date for your research proposal and a draft schedule that will allow you to meet that milestone. The timeframes for the later stages are likely to become clear later on. Like many postgraduate researchers you might want to employ a strategy known as backward mapping, working from the deadline for your research and the deadline for the research proposal.

The proposal of our example student was due at the end of the first year and she knew the exact word limit required for the proposal. Completion of the entire report was scheduled for the end of her fourth year. She knew that, as a start, she had to firm up her research questions. She could start reading the literature to find out what others had found and to identify the debates in the area. She then needed to begin writing a review of the literature to summarize and critique the findings in the literature, to identify any inconsistencies therein and to clarify where her proposed research might fit into the existing body of knowledge. The literature search involved exploring the substantive literature (the work already carried out on the topic), the theoretical literature (the work on theoretical frameworks that others employed or might have employed) and the methodological literature (the work on how others conducted their studies).

Decision-making is central to all research. For example, once the student explored these bodies of literature she could decide which theory might be appropriate to explain the data. She was also able to make a decision on how she wanted to carry out the study. With this plan in mind, she set aside time to apply for ethical clearance from her institution to carry out the project. The student also needed to communicate her many decisions to others through her research proposal. That meant she needed to build in time to write that communication.

Box 1.2   Example of an anticipated research timeline

Phase	Focus	Dates
Year 1: Phase 1 Planning and conceptualizing the research	● Finding a topic ● Developing research questions ● Understanding the relevant literature ● Demonstrating a need for the study	January–June
Year 1: Phase 2 Designing the research	● Clarifying the participants and location ● Specifying the data collection methods ● Specifying the data analysis methods ● Preparing an ethics application	July–August
Year 1: Phase 3 Preparing the research proposal	● Outlining the background to the research ● Reviewing the literature ● Outlining the research methods ● Completing the research proposal ● Contingency time allowance ● Defence of proposal	September–January
End of Planning Stages		
Year 2	Collection of data	February–December
Years 3–4	Analysis of data Final preparation of report Contingency time allowance	January–December

The level of detail described in the boxed example might be sufficient for you to work from. However, you will almost certainly be more productive if you divide your tasks into smaller chunks. Perhaps you work best from a weekly 'to-do' list. If so, you will need to develop a more detailed plan itemizing what you expect to complete each week. From your weekly schedule of tasks you might want to create a daily schedule to keep you focused and to keep you on track for successful completion. Whatever level of detail you prefer, be sure that your plan is realistic and that your goals are achievable.

Activity

TIMELINE UP TO THE RESEARCH PROPOSAL

Complete the table by adding in the time period you plan to spend on each of the activities making up the early phases of your research

Timeframe	Activity
	Finding a topic
	Developing research questions
	Understanding the relevant literature
	Demonstrating a need for the study
	Clarifying the participants and location
	Specifying the data collection methods
	Specifying the data analysis methods
	Preparing an ethics application
	Outlining the background to the research
	Reviewing the literature
	Outlining the research methods
	Completing the research proposal
	Contingency time allowance

Ethically responsible research

As a researcher, you will have ultimate control, power and influence over the ways in which you undertake your study and the kinds of outcomes that you produce. It is critical, then, that your decisions, at all stages in your research journey, are ethically informed. No research is allowed to proceed in any way that you wish just because it fulfils the purpose of meeting certain ends. Rather, you will need to consider who or what could come to harm during or because of your research. In responding to the question 'What is the morally right course of action to take as an ethical researcher?', you will employ appropriate standards and ethical norms focused on best outcomes for human beings (or birds and animals). For example, if a food scientist was interested in ice cream preferences and consumption, she would need to consider whether the volunteers in her study would be harmed in any way by sampling the quantities and kinds of ice cream under investigation.

Looking forward, decisions surrounding the recruitment of participants are made equitably and on the grounds of the participants' relationship to your research questions. You need to provide participants with full details of the research so that they are able to provide free (and not coerced) consent based on the information provided. Once the participating group is identified, you will be in a stronger position to ensure that you take the necessary steps to protect their rights. Informed consent must be obtained for all participants. Be aware that informed consent does not mean that their participation automatically continues throughout the study. Participants have the right to withdraw their involvement during any part of the study and do not need to provide reasons for their withdrawal. You will need to respect this right. As an ethical researcher, you must develop a research culture in which respect, trust and confidentiality prevail.

Your research will need to demonstrate that you have carefully thought through all aspects of the process. That means your project must have clear research goals and the design you plan must make it possible for these goals to be met. You will need to be clear on the basis for selection of your participants, and make sure that they have not been chosen to achieve a particular research objective or outcome that you have in mind. Since you will be controlling how data are collected, interpreted and selected for analysis, you must ensure that you avoid influencing the responses of your participants, and that you do not falsify or purposely exclude or destroy data. It is important to recognize that data are not owned by the researcher but rather are in the researcher's (and supervisor's) safe-keeping.

This is a good time to begin thinking about who and what might be affected, both directly and indirectly, by your proposed research. Think in terms of individuals, communities, present and future society, and so on. Each needs to be protected from harm. Benefits to them should be maximized, and all your intended practices should be principled on notions of justice. If you have identified likely harm to your participants or any individual or group that may be affected by your research, you need to consider seriously whether new research questions and a new research design might be necessary.

What you stand to gain

Right now, like many others starting out on the research journey, your excitement about undertaking research is likely to be tinged with apprehension.

> **INSIGHTS FROM A POSTGRADUATE RESEARCHER**
>
> *"At the beginning I had the feeling that doing research was really overwhelming. I felt the process was extremely challenging – certainly at the beginning – and I wondered at times whether or not I had the capabilities to manage it. Now coming out at the other end – which I almost am – I think that it's a huge source of pleasure. The satisfaction to see that, actually, I had managed it and I had managed it reasonably well, is probably the biggest pleasure."*

Take heart from those who have gone before you. You are embarking on a new journey. There are many things to learn before you succeed, but there are also many things that you will gain from the experience. You will be able to gather, interpret, synthesize and critique other researchers' ideas and findings. You will be able to design your own project to address a question that you have posed, building on current knowledge in your area of interest. You will learn how to manage the full research cycle of planning, action, learning new techniques and approaches, putting forward an argument and presenting your conclusions in an articulate way.

> **INSIGHTS FROM A POSTGRADUATE RESEARCHER**
>
> *"Research helps you develop in many different ways. Prior to undertaking my study I was not confident about standing in front of my peers and speaking. I have always been too much of a 'shrinking violet'. I was more comfortable hiding in the background and letting someone else take the limelight. Undertaking research has not allowed me to do this, and I am delighted that this has been the case. I gained confidence not only in my ability to speak in front of a crowd but also in the realization that I do actually know what I am talking about."*
>
> *"I have to say that research changed me as a person. I found out what I was really capable of. I grew as a person. The process made me aware that I am a very different person to the one I was prior to beginning the research."*

You will grow in many ways. Your information and evaluation skills may well be enhanced. You will learn how to avoid distractions that can be costly in terms of time and research quality. Perhaps your time-management skills will improve. You are likely to become more inquiring, more confident and more reflective. You may meet people with whom you would otherwise never come into contact, and as a result, you might begin to look at the world differently.

Look forward positively to the completion of the project and the huge personal satisfaction you will feel in achieving your research qualification.

Review

Main points

- Research plays an important role in society.
- Research is an organized, systematic and logical process of coming to know.
- Academic research is not simply focused on finding out facts but on offering explanations.
- Research has its own specialized vocabulary.
- There are a number of clear steps involved in the early stages of the research process.
- Research requires a number of prerequisite skills and dispositions of the researcher.
- A realistic timeline is fundamental to all research.
- All research decisions need to be ethically informed.
- Research has many academic and personal benefits for the researcher.

Key Terms

- Research timetable
- The data/theory connection
- Ethical responsibility

Looking ahead

In the next chapter the focus is on research as a field of inquiry. Chapter 2 considers how researchers go about identifying relevant and interesting issues, problems or dilemmas that might lend themselves to further exploration. Next, it looks at how to shape an area of interest into a good research topic. The chapter then explores how to make your topic manageable and researchable by creating boundaries and exclusions around it. The focus is then sharpened by looking at the stage of shaping the research question. This is a critical step in the research process since your research questions will shape all the research activity that will follow.

2 Making Early Decisions

Identifying areas of inquiry

Reported research often provides a solution to a worldwide issue. Take, for example, the issue of global warming. The research reported will typically describe how the issue has been investigated and what the research points to as a way forward. But don't for one moment think that you are expected to solve such a major contemporary challenge. No research student should aspire to this level. Rather, postgraduate researchers focus their efforts on producing a credible piece of research that advances knowledge in a small way, such as trying out something in your setting that has previously only been attempted elsewhere and, ultimately, providing a small piece of new evidence on the issue. Your contribution is likely to be significant for a very small audience and a very small academic community. It will present your own voice on the area you have chosen.

Some postgraduate researchers have the problem area already carved out for them. If your research is nested within a larger (often funded) project the area of research interest will have already been determined by the principal investigators and you will be asked, as a research student within the team, to contribute to knowledge in that area. It sometimes happens that the research team fails to make immediately clear to you where the boundary comes between your work and the work of the larger group. Take the case of Sarah who was part of a team working on a large funded project to investigate migrants' experiences. The team planned to explore a range of interests including employment and accommodation, isolation from family, language difficulties, and so forth. It wasn't until the team met to report on progress that she understood how her research contribution would be distinctive within the wider project.

If you are developing your own research project, then you are likely to already have some idea of the general area you are interested in. Francis, for example, was working towards a nursing research qualification and was scoping ideas for his project, including early childhood well-being, local community health initiatives, elder care, student mentoring within a nursing programme, youth solvent abuse, migrant health workers' professional development, and university nursing lecturers' on-line teaching. In time, it is likely that Francis will lean more towards one topic than the others, possibly because he has some prior knowledge of the specific area. He may also be aware of a potential supervisor within the institution who has expertise and knowledge relevant to that area of interest.

The point is that the area you eventually choose will not be dreamed up in a vacuum. We know from talking to postgraduate researchers that your previous experiences in higher education might also influence the direction your project will finally take. Your interests and your strengths are likely to steer you towards a specific area. Will it be a project with numbers, historical documents or events, classic literature, scientific relationships, ideas or people? Are you interested in understanding something, or working with people and making changes, or in fathoming out and explaining what is going on? Are you interested in tracking historical events? Your answers will influence the kind of research in which you will be involved.

Work and everyday experiences may well play a part in your topic decision-making but it is important to be aware of the difference between research and day-to-day life experience. While your everyday experiences are insightful, they are always seen from your personal insider's view. Simply because that view is narrow in scope on account of the context of your situation, your everyday experience may not resonate with the research literature on your topic. Since everyday experience fits the particulars of a specific situation it is likely that you already know the answers to, or can find solutions for, everyday issues or problems. Research practice, on the other hand, focuses on providing evidence that will enhance our understanding. It is a systematic way of coming to know.

You are about to set out on your new and exciting journey. Perhaps for the first time in your life – possibly for the *only* time in your life – you will have the luxury of investigating a problem or an issue over a sustained period of time. You will be able to give your attention to the task of understanding what you think is happening. You will be able to find answers to an issue that you are passionate about or will be able to come up with solutions to a problem that you find most interesting or puzzling. You will bring a fresh mind and fresh eyes to the area of interest. Postgraduate researchers tell us that selecting a topic, developing a research question and figuring out the small details of the project, then nurturing it and watching it grow are all exciting experiences. They make the decision to undertake research worthwhile.

Selecting a topic

A research topic may take some time to firm up. Of course, this can be a problem because it is likely that this is when you really want to go full steam ahead with your study. You might be clear about the general area you want to work in but may not be able to articulate just yet the specific topic you want to explore. From listening to others and from reading, there are so many interesting ideas that play on your imagination. The chances are that anyone reading your final research report will be completely oblivious to the intellectual efforts and the anxieties you experienced over the topic selection. While the topic might be clear, obvious and reasonable to you with your 20–20 hindsight later on, right now there will be seemingly endless topic possibilities to work through. Of course that observation makes the choice even more agonising. The thing to know is that the success or failure of the topic depends on what you choose to do about the topic *after* your choice is made.

The area of interest that you choose will provide a starting point for clarifying what you will do in your research. Left as it is, however, your area could lead to research in any number of directions. Some topics appear on the surface to be reasonably manageable but on closer inspection it becomes clear that it will not be possible to address the topic adequately, for reasons including the researcher's background knowledge, access to participants and necessary resources. Be assured that a research project undertaken for an academic qualification is a training ground and defining your research area is your point of entrance into the research process. Once the topic has been identified, you will want to consider the context of the study and then create boundaries around the research if you want to avoid muddling through and making needless mistakes.

But first, back to the task of identifying your topic. Tentative topic areas tend to crystallize into something workable when they align with the literature. Simply put, you won't know what to research until you have looked at the literature. Reading widely will help you clarify the research focus. As you read, and as you talk with others, unresolved non-trivial issues, specific gaps and particular areas of personal interest will begin to shine through. You will start to identify aspects of the topic that could be researched. For example, in sociology, we might want to examine what the concept of national identity means for young people. In psychology, we might want to understand the relationship between social media and youth depression. In education, you might want to explore the ways in which the achievement outcomes of Downs Syndrome students might be enhanced. Both the reading and the revisiting of the initial research area are crucial to the process of finally deciding on the topic and identifying the context of the research. It's an iterative process – you start with a hunch of what you want to do, you read around that topic, you revisit your research focus, you read more, you come up with a specific context for the study – and you carry on until you are satisfied that you have come up with what you want to focus on in your research.

Reading and thinking about the literature in relation to your topic are critical stages in the planning of your research. Having a command of what is happening in your topic area will allow the focus of your study to emerge and be redefined. Remember that clarification and refining of the research topic takes time and may seem to unnecessarily delay progress with the research. But it is time well spent. Factors to consider when selecting a topic grounded in the literature relate to size, scope, time, resources, skill, and access. A good research topic is one that is

- clearly and closely defined,
- significant and timely,
- suited to your skills and expertise, time and the resources at hand,
- able to be researched.

Once you learn the skills of refining your chosen topic and making it researchable and manageable, then it is a simple step to state your research aim.

Karen was confident that her research topic was exactly the one that would keep her motivated through the research period. She had been concerned about her employees' well-being for some time and a topic like this, which was very close to her heart, would be sure to sustain her interest. She was confident that it did have real substance and was likely to have

---

Case Study 2.1

LOOKING AT POSSIBLITIES FOR KAREN'S TOPIC

Karen was interested in the research area of *obesity*. She wasn't clear in her mind exactly what she wanted to research. She hoped that the literature would give her some inspiration but found that many of the studies on obesity in the literature seemed removed from her own knowledge of the area and her personal experiences and dispositions. She found, for example, reports of studies on obesity levels amongst different social groups; factors associated with the development of obesity; living with obesity; the effect of obesity on memory, emotions and appetite; change processes in relation to obesity; medical prevention of obesity; treatment of obesity; social attitudes to childhood obesity; health-related implications of obesity; and environmental obesity. There were others, too, but none of these connected with her experience and concerns in her role as manager of a large company office. Karen thought about the workers in her company whose responsibilities included data entry onto computer files. She considered many of these employees to be overweight. She wondered if she could introduce a health and fitness programme into the workplace and find out what the effects on the workers might be.

direct benefits for the employees and, in the longer term, for her company. She knew that she would need to learn new skills along the way and was looking forward to the challenge. There was nothing she could see in her topic that was unfeasible or unrealistic and was confident that she had the resources, time and, of course, access to her participants. But she wondered if she might be too close to the topic, and decided to talk over the aspect of feasibility with her supervisor, with a view towards making some adjustments if necessary. As it turned out, the supervisor was encouraging and at that stage Karen converted her ideas into the research objective: 'To explore the effects of a workplace health and well-being initiative on workers' sense of self and productivity'.

Bill has an interest in the area of teacher effectiveness. He might decide to explore that area through an historical survey, looking at changes in the way effectiveness has been defined over time. Or he might like to hear what teachers, principals or students have to say about teacher effectiveness. Then again, he might be interested in tracking an initiative for positive changes to teachers' effectiveness in a specific learning environment. Or perhaps he might want to identify at close quarters precisely what an effective teacher does over an extended period. The possibilities for this topic are too numerous to name.

Bill fairly quickly decided that a linear approach, like that used by Karen, was not allowing him to make much progress. Undaunted, he took pen to paper and brainstormed everything that came into his mind about teacher effectiveness. Finally, after many attempts, Bill found that his approach identified a number of closely-contained areas of interest, which he grouped together on the mind-map. Every entry seemed to approach the topic from a different perspective, and Bill knew that his interest would definitely not be sustained if he tried to follow a number of the pathways. Deep down, he wanted to be able to explain to others what effective teaching looks like, but it wasn't until he undertook the mind-map exercise that he was able to see it clearly. Bill had personal experience with teaching secondary students and decided that the secondary sector could be interesting to study. He started jotting down a few ideas and found that as he read, talked to others, and thought more about his topic he was able to add to his mind-map. Finally, he put all these perspectives into the chart shown in Case Study 2.2.

Talking about your research with others is another way in which you can clarify for yourself the key features of what you are planning. It forces you to consider the big picture rather than the small detail. It enables you to consider the value of your proposed research and why you might be planning to undertake it. How will you know you have convinced your acquaintance of what you are planning? You will know from their response and the questions they ask. Try the activity opposite until you consider you have successfully attained the 'research topic in three sentences' status.

Case Study 2.2

BILL'S MIND-MAP FOR TEACHER EFFECTIVENESS

Teachers' qualifications
Teachers' professional learning

What sector?
early childhood
primary school
secondary school

How is 'effective' measured?
raising students' academic achievements
enhancing students' social outcomes
developing critical thinking

When? What era?
effectiveness now?
effectiveness some time ago?

Whose views?
teachers
students
parents
principals
curriculum policy
media
others?

What happens in the classroom?
instructing
questioning
selecting tasks and activities
developing a classroom comunity
responding to students
noticing and listerning
using hands-on equipment and technology
assessing knowledge
anything else?

Other relationships
colleagues
school principal
parents and wider community
media

Activity

RESEARCH TOPIC IN THREE SENTENCES

1. Identify your research area.
2. Using either the mind map or the linear approach illustrated in Case Studies 2.1 and 2.2, list at least three possible topics that could be researched within your research area.
3. Clarify your own topic within the research area.
4. Now imagine you are at a social function and an acquaintance asks you to explain what your research topic is about. In *three* sentences, explain the research you are planning.

   To assist you in the task:

   ● Focus on the absolute essentials.

   ● Avoid jargon and unfamiliar terminology.

   ● Keep your explanation at a conversational level.

Developing the research question

Now that you are clear about your research topic you need to sharpen the
focus and clarify precisely what it is that you want to find out. The way of
doing this within research is to pose questions which you will subsequently
attempt to answer. In other words, your research questions define what you
are trying to discover through your research activity. They make it possible
for others to understand precisely what you plan to do and what you want
to find out. They set sharp boundaries around and guide a focused research
investigation. Regardless of the kind of research you are planning, you need
to provide a research question if you want to understand things better and
find out how and why processes and practices work or do not work. If your
question is not formulated in a way that allows you to find answers, then you
will not be able to make a contribution to the topic area. Some researchers
believe that the research question may be the most important part of the
research. If you come up with a good research question, then you are likely
to be on the right track to producing a good piece of research.

In my view, the ability to formulate a good research question is one of
the most important skills that a researcher needs. It is also possibly the most
difficult skill required of you during your research. You must ask the right
kind of question. Postgraduate researchers sometimes make the mistake
in thinking that 'good' research questions should be written in highly academic jargon. This is not the case. In fact a clear, simple research question is
infinitely better than one that no-one really understands. In addition, some
postgraduate researchers confuse the 'research question' with the 'interview question'. Let's be clear from the start: we are *not* talking here of the
questions you might want to ask your participants in an interview later on.
Interview questions are tools for gathering data. The research question, on
the other hand, defines what your entire research activity is focused on finding out. The research question will, of course, be non-trivial: it will require
considerable thought and analysis to answer it. You will need to be sure that
it can be researched, given your specific circumstances, including the time
and resources you have at hand.

Researchable questions are specific and limited in scope. They narrow
down the big areas of interest to something much more manageable. They
might explore the nature of a relationship between variables. The fewer the
main research questions, the better. For example, your general area of interest might be in investigating the effects of daylight saving on participation in
sport. An area of interest like this is far too broad to guide a research study.
A more limited and specific question is needed, for example: 'What is the
nature of young working people's recreational sporting activities during the
first month of daylight saving compared with young people's recreational

sporting activities during the month before daylight saving begins?' Sub-questions that follow logically from this primary research question will focus your study even further.

The fascinating thing is that every research purpose asks a different kind of research question. What is going on? What is the solution? How can this be explained more clearly? How can this be improved? How effective is this? Each kind of question provides direction and sets limits on your research. Each also points to a different kind of research design (Fraenkel and Wallen, 2008). If you are embarking on a theoretical or philosophical research programme then your research questions will be open and exploratory and you may not be clear at this stage what might eventuate from your study. However, if you expect your programme of study to provide straightforward answers to your questions, then you will need to gather evidence that can be observed, measured, touched or counted. This is what is meant by empirical research.

Postgraduate researchers tend to forget that empirical research can only deal with the observable and measurable aspects of a question. Moral questions, as well as issues relating to aesthetics, fashion, etiquette, religious faith and political ideology, cannot be answered. However, with careful adjustments, they can be reformulated into researchable questions. For example, the question 'Is St Peter's Basilica in Rome more or less captivating than the Taj Mahal?'cannot be answered by research. However, it could be converted into an empirical question: 'How many fourth-year students believe that St Peter's is more beautiful than the Taj Mahal?'

Typically, research questions evolve and shift during the beginning stages of research. In some situations you may need to change or modify them during the course of the study. However, once the research question (and any sub-questions) have finally been firmed up, it is important that your research does not stray or shift away from answering them. Indeed the research question will provide direction for everything you do in your study. In other words, all your research activity needs to be fully focused on finding answers to the research question that you have developed. From the literature you read to the data you collect, and the methods you use to analyze the data – all must match what you have determined needs to be addressed. What is more, when you come to write your conclusions you will return to the research question. In so many ways your research starts and ends with the research question. It gives your research coherence. That is why it is so very important to get the research question right.

Bill's area of interest, as we saw earlier, was teacher effectiveness. Looking at his mind-map Bill soon realized that he wanted to be able to explain to others what effective teaching looks like. From that decision he was able to eliminate a number of approaches to the topic, including a historical investigation, people's perceptions, a 'change' project, a scientific experiment and an evaluation study. He hoped that he could track what an effective teacher does in the classroom over an extended period of time. He wanted to set some boundaries for his research and decided that all the things that a teacher does in the classroom could be summarized as developing a community of learners. Initially, he thought he would explore what teachers from different schools do with effect in their classrooms so that he could make a few tentative generalizations.

Bill's first attempt at a research question was: What does effective teaching look like? After spending time thinking about this question he decided that it seemed too broad and too loose for his main objective. It would not enable him to get to the 'nitty gritty' of what an effective teacher does. Narrowing the scope of his research at a number of levels (numbers of teachers, specific classes, grade level) he decided to focus his research on one teacher during a mathematics class at the grade 12 level. His research objective became: To explore the ways in which one effective teacher develops a community of learners in a grade 12 mathematics classroom. The objective led him to develop a more refined research question: What are the characteristics of effective teaching in a grade 12 middle-set mathematics classroom?

Karen, who we met earlier, had acquired some useful facts and figures about obesity from her initial pass through the literature. She also found a number of helpful reports on studies undertaken in the workplace. After much deliberating, she decided that she wanted to focus on her own workplace. She was not interested so much in describing and explaining what went on in the workplace as on changing the environment. She reasoned that if she could effect a change of attitude towards health and well-being within the workplace environment, then the findings would directly impact on the company, as well as on the individual workers. The research aim she finally developed was to explore the effects of a workplace health and well-being initiative on workers' sense of self and productivity. Turning the research aim into a research question led her to: What are the effects of a health and well-being initiative on workplace productivity and personal well-being?

Both Bill and Karen produced very specific questions. Bill narrowed his focus to one teacher and one class and the way in which he taught that class. The question suggests that Bill is going to explore teaching effectiveness through a long and close 'look' at what the teacher does. He might observe lessons, he might interview the teacher at different points of time, he might video-record lessons and ask the teacher to view the recording and explain why he chose a specific action and a specific communication with the students. He might look at the teacher's lessons plans and other classroom documentation that could provide evidence of effectiveness. We do not know immediately what the answer to Bill's research question will be, but we might speculate that there could be many facets to what Bill finds out about effective teaching.

Similarly, for Karen's research, we do not know what answer her research question will yield. There could well be positive effects, but we will not know if our hunch is correct, or what the positive (or negative) effects are, until the research has taken place. What Karen needed for her research was a dataset that would allow her to measure or assess her workers' health, well-being and productivity before and after the initiative took place. The interesting thing was that, once Karen had formulated her research question, much of the deliberation over what kinds of data to gather was taken out of her hands. The key point is that the research question has the effect of sharpening the research focus and points the researcher in a direction for the data collection.

Situating the research within a worldview

Every piece of academic research is based on a worldview. Different worldviews are linked to different assumptions. For example, if a tourist from the United Kingdom were to visit a remote Papua New Guinea community, it is unlikely that his or her Western worldview would be the same as that of the local people. The tourist's understanding of what constitutes the community is likely to comprise the countable numbers of people within the environs of that village. On the other hand, a member of the Papua New Guinea community might understand it as comprising the people readily identifiable 'on the ground', together with those who have moved to other community sites as well as members of the community who have died. The assumptions that relate to the nature of reality can be aligned with assumptions concerning valid knowledge of that reality. The community member might take it for granted, and may not be able to articulate, that he or she knows all those people are 'there' because their presence is felt in everything the community does. The tourist might defer to the seeing, touching or hearing aspects relating to the presence of community members.

In the same way, in academic research, the student buys into a set of assumptions that fits a particular worldview. Research never happens in a vacuum. The researcher's worldview always underpins the topic and the research question. To emphasize that point, Karen's and Bill's respective worldviews sent them down particular pathways, (implicitly) guiding the direction of their research. They both made a number of assumptions about the form and nature of the reality being studied and made another set of assumptions about appropriate ways of developing knowledge of that reality. That is to say, they made assumptions based on a worldview about the kind of research to be undertaken, the kind of research question to be posed, and the kinds of methods that might be proposed for studying the topic under investigation.

Different worldviews generate different theories. Worldviews are some-times referred to as paradigms of knowledge, and are the means through which we come to understand research. It is important that the way we go about research, as well as the findings the research produces, are sit-uated within and viewed through particular paradigms. For example, Bill was drawn to the theory of socio-culturalism. The theory seemed to match his worldview and he hoped that it would help him explain from his data what an effective teacher does in the classroom. Karen preferred to take a community of practice approach. Another researcher might lean towards a theory that provided a way of illustrating how changed workplace policies construct and regulate the kind of person that a worker might become. Yet another researcher exploring the same topic might be drawn to activity the-ory to explain aspects of the work and its interconnections to other aspects that are undertaken daily in the workplace. Still another researcher might be drawn to information-processing psychology to explain a dataset from the work being carried out in the workplace. All these points of theoretical difference help the researcher think, imagine, ask questions and explain data in a specific way.

Theory is a sharp instrument for framing your study and for interacting with the data at a level beyond mere description. You need to be aware that the theoretical frames we use to make sense of events and practices have consequences for how we go about research. The kinds of questions that we might ask, even down to the questioning itself, and the kinds of data we might collect for our study stem from the theories that guide our understanding about how we claim to know what we know. They offer a way of interpreting the world. Researchers may draw on different theories to emphasize some aspects of the topic more than others, putting bounda-ries around the scope of the research. The theoretical lens employed will serve as a starting point for a formalized set of propositions that explain *why* things happen as they do. In all the approaches to, for example, a workplace study, as in any other research, the researcher will use theory to both de-scribe the data and to build explanations about the observations.

Defining key concepts

Tom was planning on exploring the work of elite sports coaches. He started with the big question: 'What coaching practices do elite athletes perceive as conducive to their individual development as an athlete?' We can make the relationship between coaching practice and individual development, which is implied in the question, researchable by working through a few steps.

Case Study 2.3

TOM'S RESEARCH

Sport and recreation

Tom was a keen sportsman and wanted to understand how sports teams operate successfully at the national representative level. In his own sporting activities at a lower level he had experienced a wide range of coaching strategies and found that some had 'worked' better than others. He wondered if he could identify specific coaching actions, talk and behaviours to which elite sportsmen responded positively. He was particularly interested in finding out which types of coaching were effective in enhancing individual team members' athletic development.

Tom provided the following research overview:

Topic: Coaching practices within elite sports

Aim: To explore coaching practices deemed productive for elite athletes' individual development.

Research question: What coaching practices do elite athletes perceive as conducive to their individual development as an athlete?

Boundaries: One national representative male sports team; two coaching locations; period of three months; observations at all coaching sessions; observations of interactions between coach and team members in social events and in travel to match site; interviews with team members.

First, we need to be more specific about our key concepts.

● How will we define coaching practices? Do we focus on what the coach does on the field? Do we include 'pep' talks during a match, as well as expressions of congratulations and commiserations at the end of a match? What about other interactions between coach and team members during travel to and from a sports event?

● How do we define elite athletes? Will they necessarily be sportspeople who represent a national team? If not, what do we mean by 'elite'?

The answers to these questions will engender more focused considerations:

● What sport?
● When will this research take place?
● Over what period of time will we investigate the coaching practices?
● Will the coaching be focused towards winning a significant match?
● What location(s)?
● Will our elite sportspeople be male or female?

If you have a hunch that there might be a relationship between coaching practices for the chosen sport and gender then you might want to create further boundaries around the question.

We apply the same kind of probes to the issue of individual development.

- What do we mean by individual development? Athleticism? Probably. Cognitive development? Probably not. Social skills? A sense of team identity and belonging? Health and well-being? Exhibiting commonly held values, such as respect for others, tolerance, fairness?
- What theoretical basis exists for these decisions?

When Tom answers the last two questions he will be able to clarify what he wants to include and what he wants to exclude in 'individual development'. He will start to create greater specificity around his research question. He will then be in a strong position to defend his choice of indicators and, eventually, to find answers. Be aware, however, that narrowing the research question does not always mean that the question will be more easily answered.

Case Study 2.4

MICHELLE'S RESEARCH

Guidance counselling

Michelle was working toward a guidance counselling research qualification. She was particularly interested in grief counselling and, in her work, had worked with a few families who had lost a young child. She had found the experience challenging and considered that other counsellors may have had similar experiences. She wanted to carry out research that explored what other counsellors do. She hoped that the research might yield ideas for good practice which she could use to create an inventory for counsellors.

Michelle set out the bare bones of her research in this way:

Topic: Grief counselling.

Aim: To explore good practice and to develop an inventory of useful ways for counsellors to guide parents through grief following the death of a young child.

Research question: What practices and processes do grief counsellors undertake to assist parents who are suffering from the loss of their young child?

Boundaries: Grief counselling; five grief counsellors who have assisted parents following the death of a young child; large urban location; interviews. No observations of practice because of ethical considerations.

In a similar way to Tom, Michelle will need to define her key concepts. Pulling apart one of her key terms, we might ask:

- What does Michelle mean by grief counselling?
- How do official statements within the profession define the concept?
- Does Michelle want to vary the official definition and sharpen it in some way?
- Does she mean counselling that the client will pay for and is, therefore, able to choose the counsellor?
- Or, is this counselling to be paid for by a government service and hence, likely to imply that there will be limited or no choice over counsellor?
- How many hours counselling will be involved for each person?

These other questions will need to be asked to clarify exactly how counselling is defined. A few more words that are central to her planned research need unpacking. We will apply the same probing process to 'parents'.

- Does she mean one or two?
- Caregiver(s)?
- And what do we understand by 'young child'?
- Could the 'death' be sudden? Accidental? Resulting from a long-term medical condition?

Once Michelle clarifies her key concepts, her supervisors and the readers of her proposal and final report will all be 'on the same page'. If Michelle decides to reduce the scope of grief counselling available to 'private service fee-paying, and 'young child's death' to 'death from a long-term medical condition of children between three and six years of age' then she has considerably sharpened her research focus.

When you begin to think at the conceptual level you are starting to think like a researcher. This is a good time to embark on the serious task of clarifying, sharpening and providing greater specificity around your own work.

Activity

MY MAIN RESEARCH OBJECTIVES AND QUESTIONS

Consider the main objectives and the research questions of your proposed work.
1. What key constructs/terms/concepts are relevant to your work?
   (e.g., elite sportspeople/grief counselling/systems/identity/power/ relationships…)
2. Consider a possible theory that would help you explain and analyze those concepts in the context of your work.

The conceptual framework

You are now beginning to think like a researcher. You have made decisions on fundamental aspects of your research. You have brought a worldview into your research and you may also have obtained some understanding of how the phenomena you want to study could be explained. You have clarified your research areas and identified your specific topic. Once you had created a number of boundaries around your topic, you were able to formulate a research question to which you think you can find an answer. You tightened up the scope even more by defining the concepts that will be central to your research. The decisions that you made on all these aspects form the backbone to what you plan to do. The interesting thing is that all these decisions are connected and interrelated.

Sometimes the obvious escapes our view, so we will look at the connections in Michelle's proposed research (Case Study 2.4). Michelle already knows quite a lot about counselling from her work as a counsellor and from her academic course. This prior knowledge establishes a worldview and provides her with theories about counselling which will permeate through all the decisions she makes. Her choice of grief counselling and her interest in best practice both influence the kind of research question she might formulate. They also impact on the participants and the methods for data collection that she might consider in her research. It is, for example, most unlikely that her participants would include school counsellors. Equally, because she wants to explore good practice, it is not likely that she will formulate a question relating to the family's experiences resulting from the loss of a young child. Although she might find that issue very interesting – and she may admit that she could become easily side-tracked reading about it in the literature – given her specific focus she will not be able to explore it in this research.

Like Michelle, you may be tempted to go off on a tangent and read about any number of fascinating studies that you could explore further. A conceptual framework (Leshem and Trafford, 2007) will help keep you focused. It will provide you with a coherent plan for your research and should ensure that you make decisions with careful thought and justification. It will help to establish connections between all the aspects of your proposed research. To summarize, a conceptual framework will demonstrate that your research has conceptual integrity – an interrelationship between the purpose of your research and the formulation of a relevant and realistic research question, the information and data needed, the ways in which you will collect and analyze the data, the numbers and specific participants in your study, and how you might report the findings.

The conceptual framework you develop will be unique to you and your research at this particular point in time and this particular stage of your planning. Interestingly, if you had developed a conceptual framework when you were first considering undertaking research, the framework would probably have been much more complex than the one you might develop at this stage. At the beginning, as in Bill's research in our Case Study 2.2 example, you were not absolutely clear of what you would research. You might have jotted down everything that came to mind, as long as it was relevant to the broader research topic and, if you had taken the time to consider how the elements might be connected, you might have begun to appreciate the complexity of the relationships. Perhaps you also became aware that there were multiple research projects involved. Now that you have now given careful consideration to the topic and the research question, both of which have pointed you in a specific direction for selecting your participants and your research methods, your conceptual framework will be simpler and you will be able to see the interrelationships between elements more clearly.

Case Study 2.2 presented Bill's mind-map for his research. Bill made the decision to explore the ways in which one effective teacher develops a community of learners in a grade 12 mathematics classroom. The research question he developed was: What are the characteristics of effective teaching in a grade 12 mathematics classroom? Case Study 2.5 overleaf shows the conceptual framework he constructed from the mind-map he developed when brainstorming ideas. He added 'mathematics' and 'grade 12 class', eliminated 'early childhood' and 'primary school', and decided not to pursue the views of students, parents and principals. He felt that the inclusion of teachers' professional learning and school–home and school–community links broadened the research too widely and so he eliminated those aspects too. He thought that the position that the media took on effective teaching might provide useful background material and, since he was drawn to socio-cultural explanations of teaching and learning, both social student outcomes, as well as academic outcomes, were obvious inclusions. He merged critical thinking as an aspect of academic outcomes. Once he had put these boundaries around the study he knew what was going to be explored and what was not going to be explored. That is to say, he now knew that, in his study of effective mathematics teaching, not every activity that the teacher uses in daily teaching practice would be studied, and not every single connection that the teacher has with others through teaching would be examined.

In effect, Bill had refined his research question in relation to his world-view. He had probed and redefined the concepts that he wished to use. These concepts clarified what he knew already about teacher effectiveness and left room for exploring what he did not know. He then took his conceptual framework to his supervisor to provide an outline of the abstract ideas, and their interrelationships as linked through his chosen theoretical perspective. He wanted to give the supervisor a basic structure of what, who, and for how

Case Study 2.5

BILL'S CONCEPTUAL FRAMEWORK FOR RESEARCH ON TEACHER EFFECTIVENESS

National curriculum statements on teaching and learning
↓
School policies on teaching and learning – Principal/school board
↓
Maths department policies on teaching and learning
↓
Teacher's teaching experiences
Teacher's qualifications
Teacher's views of teaching and learning
Teacher's professional learning experiences
↓
Teacher's classroom practices in a grade 12
middle-set mathematics class
planning
instructing
selecting tasks and activities
responding to students' questioning
using hands-on equipment and technology
assessing understanding
others?
↓
Raising students' academic achievements
Enhancing students' social outcomes

long, he wanted to research. He hoped that the framework might convince her that this would be a worthwhile and feasible piece of research. In a sense, in developing a conceptual framework for his proposed work, Bill was also developing an intellectual argument to justify the decisions he had made.

Activity

MY CONCEPTUAL FRAMEWORK

Consider your own research.
Develop your own conceptual framework, outlining the key concepts and illustrating any interrelationships.

Review

Main points

- Your interests and your strengths are likely to steer you towards a specific area of inquiry.
- It takes time to firm up a topic and make it researchable and manageable.
- Reading and talking with others will help you clarify your research topic.
- Good research topics are clearly and closely defined, they are significant and suited to the researcher's skills, available time and resources, and it is possible to research them.
- Researchers pose research questions which they subsequently attempt to answer.
- The formulation of good research questions is one of the most important stages in the research process.
- The concepts that you plan to use need to be clearly defined.
- A conceptual framework illustrates the coherence of your plan and provides justification for your research.

Key Terms

- Areas of inquiry
- The research topic
- The research question
- Concepts
- Conceptual framework

Looking ahead

The next chapter will widen the focus to look at the literature. The literature has an important purpose in all academic research and will help you to contextualize your own study. The literature sources at your disposal are varied and can be found in a wide range of places. The chapter will look at the relative merits of using each of these different sources. It will draw on the notion of the conceptual framework to search for the literature, using key terms. New search strategies and an efficient way to organize and manage your literature sources will be discussed. All literature that is used in research needs to be critiqued and we will look at a framework for that evaluation.

3 Gathering and Evaluating Relevant Literature

The purpose of the literature

Research involves a lot of decisions and you have already made a number that will be of major significance for your research. The specific topic has been decided and questions have been developed. In a systematic way, you identified a number of concepts that provide an opportunity for you to explore what you do not know about your topic. You then developed a conceptual framework to reveal the way in which chosen concepts are interrelated in the proposed research. The literature played a part in making these decisions – an initial reading of the literature helped clarify how your research might proceed.

The literature is now going to take on a bigger role in your research. To date, your reading has been helpful in informing you of the debates centred on your area of interest, it has clarified what is being discussed and what has been found or achieved in relation to your topic. From your reading you have cultivated an intuitive understanding of the subject. Now the literature will assist you in understanding your topic and research problem more acutely. In examining the literature more deeply and widely, you will become more informed of what is happening in your topic area.

Through searching the literature you gain insight into the key themes, concepts, issues, trends, practices, theories and methodological approaches that are commonly used in addressing your topic. You might also become aware of related areas of interest such as policies and laws that might assist you in answering your research question. Importantly, you will develop an understanding of any major controversies related to the topic and an interpretation of any inconsistencies in reported findings. Once you have a command of your chosen topic, you will begin to appreciate where you might make a contribution to knowledge. On the other hand, your wider reading might point to where your research objectives, research questions or conceptual framework might need to be modified. What you read from the literature will influence the specific direction your research will take.

A key purpose of the literature is to contexualize your own research. In that sense, the literature search is an essential activity in the research process. It is an indispensable way of developing expertise and credibility within your topic area. Searching through the literature enables you to build on the work of others. You need to establish how you might anchor your own work within the discussions and debates that are already taking place. You will not be able to make a worthwhile contribution to knowledge if your research is situated on the fringe of current arguments. Nor will you be able to contribute to those debates if you simply reproduce what others have already done. Providing a research focus that is explicitly linked to the current debate will allow you to join in the intellectual conversation, and having a voice in those conversations means that you will be able to make a contribution to knowledge.

Having a voice will allow you to demonstrate how your research will be compatible with, yet differ from, work that has already been undertaken. Some researchers talk of this process as identifying the gaps in existing work – asking questions that have not yet been addressed or have not yet been resolved in an adequate manner, or posing the same questions for a different setting. By connecting your research to the existing body of knowledge you create a rationale for your study. But not only that, by engaging with the literature you begin to see themes, methods, even additional or alternative questions, and the possibilities for analyzing your own data, all of which might otherwise have escaped your attention. In many ways, engagement with the literature is foundational to your research and is what you are really aiming for.

Reading and evaluating the literature relevant to your chosen topic provides the basis for the literature review in your research report or thesis. It is important to be aware that good research is judged in relation to a particular existing and up-to-date body of knowledge. The literature review will enable you to draw on themes that are readily recognizable and it will also provide scope for you to use terms in ways that are similar or at odds with the ways in which they are used by other researchers. In many ways, the quality of your research hinges on your reading. It will enable you to demonstrate that you are aware of the debates that are circulating within your professional community and the themes that have been explored previously. But most of all, the literature review will help you to determine how you can make a contribution to those debates and themes.

Case Study 3.1

MARTIN'S RESEARCH

The impact on perceptions of self within community 'do-it-yourself' environments

EXPLORING THE LITERATURE

Martin was aware that in some small communities in his country a number of 'handy-man' environments for males had been established by community service groups. He had visited one in a large building and found that the attendees were retired and older men with varying levels of experience in handy-man activities. They used the tools and materials provided by local businesses and individuals in order to repair items, or to work on their own project or on a community project such as repairing items for people in retirement villages or making toys for children with disabilities.

Martin was interested in how these groups operated, and especially wanted to know whether the environments had any impact on the self-concept of the attendees. He had developed that interest from observing the men's apparent enjoyment from chatting and sharing stories or simply having a cup of tea or coffee with others.

Martin's initial pass through the literature did not shed much light on any research in this specific environment, but he did find a broad-ranging literature base on formal, informal and non-formal learning hubs. From that literature he was able to formulate his research questions and key concepts. His conceptual framework led to a body of literature that theorized communities of learning, as well as literature that reported on empirical studies with specific themes such as male support, nurturance and care, apprenticeship learning models. It also led him to local policies on community activities. His more focused reading centred on studies that had explored the impact on participants in non-formal learning environments.

Types of literature

Before you can begin to consider how you might make a contribution to the current debates you will need to retrieve material for your more focused reading. You already have an overview of the topic and have familiarized yourself with the general area. From the few sources that you have assembled you have gained a general sense of the work that has already been carried out in your chosen area. Now you want to know where to search for material that relates directly to your topic and research questions. Since the available literature might prove to be overwhelming in terms of quantity and type, you need to set realistic targets concerning the number and kind of sources that would be appropriate for the qualification you are working towards.

There are essentially two sources of information: primary and secondary. Both sources of academic work will both provide you with information, but you need to be clear about the origins of the information. The relative emphasis on the two types of source will depend on your discipline.

Primary sources – information that you gain from original materials. The sources provide direct evidence or first-hand testimony in relation to the topic and are produced by the researchers or witnesses themselves. In the case of a journal article, the primary source usually represents the first reporting of a piece of research. Since they are original sources they have not been interpreted or altered. Primary sources include journal articles, original documents, diaries, artefacts, annual reports, a recording, a constitution, photographs, letters and archival material.

Secondary sources – information that you gain from third parties on research that has already been carried out. Since these channels often provide a comprehensive overview of studies that have been undertaken in relation to your topic, they may be most useful during the early stages of the literature search. Secondary sources include review papers, commentaries, reference lists, bibliographies, media reports reporting on other research and databases. It is important to appreciate that in postgraduate research, secondary accessions must be sourced from academic work.

In searching for primary and secondary sources, you will be able to take advantage of a wide range of information repositories. They include journals, books, edited volumes and chapters, monographs, textbooks, handbooks, theses and dissertations, legislation and policy, government publications, national archives, professional journals, newspapers and magazines, grey literature and informal channels. We shall look at each of these separately.

Journals contain a rich source of evidence, using varied methodological approaches, from empirical studies. They also showcase new theoretical developments. They are generally considered to reflect contemporary high quality focused research. Journal articles are available in either printed or electronic form; often in both. Journals tend to have focused interests and these include reporting on research at the international, national or local level.

Books are available in printed and electronic form. Book publishers build in quality control mechanisms but these processes are not considered as robust as those in place for peer-reviewed journals. Single or jointly authored books report cohesively and with consistent quality on a topic.

Edited volumes and their chapters focus on a specific topic from a range of viewpoints and approaches. Chapters are often useful sources of information for the new researcher. However, the quality may not always be consistent from one chapter to another within an edited volume.

Monographs are scholarly pieces of published work. They explore a single topic or a few related topics through the presentation of an academic argument. Many monographs are adaptations of a doctoral thesis. As a consequence they demonstrate a higher level of detail, analysis and rigour than is often associated with books.

Textbooks provide overviews of a topic and often engage readers at a basic level. They tend to offer the reader an introduction to seminal studies rather than to contemporary work being undertaken on the topic. The level of analysis is lower than evidenced in other scholarly works.

Handbooks provide state-of-the-art information relating to a specific topic or a range of topics. In disciplines where handbooks are available, they tend to be published in large volumes and at regular intervals. They typically consist of a series of chapters, each of which is a collaborative effort of experts in the area.

Theses and dissertations are usually available in the library of the university at which the research degree was undertaken. National and international databases and specialist bibliographies index theses and make them available for searching. Theses offer an often overlooked rich source of information on a topic for the new researcher, and will invariably dedicate a full chapter to the literature.

Legislation and policy publications offer the new researcher a range of legal documents to help build a case for research or for critical commentary. These documents and papers can be retrieved from appropriate websites and from university libraries.

Government publications are useful sources of information for contextualizing a topic. These may include directives from a department or ministry on an issue. They may include discussions on legislation or policy and may also contain reports of research findings. In some countries these publications can be downloaded or ordered from ministry or government departmental websites. Some are stored in university libraries.

National archives store a wide range of material that will be particularly useful to the new researcher planning historical research and possibly for researchers planning other kinds of research. For example, in some projects records of debates within legislative bodies such as the Senate, the House of Representatives, or Parliament, as well as influential historical reports and records, may be crucial to the contextualization of the study.

Professional journals provide direction in relation to recent legislation, policies and practice. They also offer contemporary viewpoints about current issues for the professional group. The information within professional journals can sometimes be retrieved through websites.

Newspapers and magazines reflect contemporary views and information about a topic and interpret recent events. In those respects, they may be useful to the new researcher. However, the quality control systems for newspaper and magazine articles are not as robust as those for academic articles.

Grey Literature is defined as material that is not published through conventional sources but through specialized centres. The material may take the form of reports, conference papers or similar, and may be produced by, for example, a community body, a voluntary group or a sporting organization. While the quality is untested, the information provided may prove to be highly relevant to your topic.

Informal channels may include a wide range of communication. For example, supervisors, colleagues, friends, family members and acquaintances may pass on useful information around the topic.

There are so many places for you to find your literature. In academic work, peer-reviewed journals are generally considered more favourably as sources of evidence, and of quality, than many other sources. Whether the journal's scope relates to subject specialty or to interdisciplinary work, the peer-review process that most journals demand provides an assurance that the articles represent reliable sources of information. Be aware that there is a hierarchy of journals, measured by its impact score. The impact score is a measure of citation. For example, a high impact score of just over or around 1 means that every paper published in the high-ranking journal has been cited one or more times within five years by another paper in a range of given journals. Another indicator is the list of distinguished names on the editorial board. Papers in high-ranking journals do tend to carry more status.

Because of the status of journals within academic work, some postgraduate researchers believe that only peer-reviewed and high-ranking articles should be accessed during the literature search. However, supervisors and examiners would argue for the inclusion of other sources of information. While international literature published in journals may be important, it is also essential that you source material from your literature search that is local and national. Overlooking significant local or national literature will not sit favourably with examiners. A wide range of appropriate sources offers your work a more comprehensive and richer literature base for your research.

Activity

SOURCING MY LITERATURE

Consider your topic and the research questions of your proposed work.

1. What are the key government websites you might search for relevant information?
2. How might you go about locating potentially useful 'grey literature'?
3. What key websites provide national datasets of information relevant to your topic?
4. What key websites provide access to professional associations relevant to your topic?

Search strategies

By the time you enrol in a postgraduate research qualification, your information literacy skills will be reasonably well developed. It is highly likely that you will know how to navigate your way through the volumes of information available on the web to access legislation and policy documents, government publications, national archival information and professional journals, as well as newspaper reports and magazines and what we have called 'grey literature'. Not all of these sources, of course, will be relevant to your topic. If any of the sources essential to your work are not readily available on the web, you will need to consider what alternative avenues you could use to access them.

Similar search strategies are used for locating information in journals, books, edited volumes, monographs, textbooks, handbooks, as well as theses and dissertations. These sources are best searched through your university's library site which will make it possible for you to search on-line for resources at the time of the day or night that is most convenient to you.

If you are not familiar with library searches, then the best person to approach is a university librarian. He or she is also your best source of advice if you want assistance on a specific problem or if you simply want reassurance that you are assembling the appropriate literature or using the right approach. It is quite likely that your university library has assigned a liaison librarian to assist postgraduate researchers in your discipline area. Spare yourself the personal dramas of searching unproductively and seek assistance from the person whose career centres around a commitment to information literacy.

Librarians are the postgraduate researchers' best friends. Make a one-to-one appointment either face-to-face or on-line, whichever is most convenient. The librarian's knowledge will lead you to accessing material that you would never have been able to locate on your own. They know where to find obscure unpublished material, reports and bibliographies, and so forth. They also keep up to date with the new acquisitions in the library and once they know you and your topic, they will be able to pass this information on to you. They will also assist you in locating relevant theses and research reports, help you use the interlibrary loan system for material your library does not hold, as well as help you set up journal alerts by which you are informed through email of the latest issues of your selected journals.

Perhaps more importantly, the librarian will be able to help develop your understanding of database protocols and the construction of search strategies. You are aiming to learn how to conduct a systematic investigation of a number of bibliographic databases. Your investigation will need to search through more than one dataset, principally because not every individual journal will appear in a single database. When you carry out an investigation successfully you are navigating effectively and efficiently through large numbers of journals and through references to a number of books, reports and websites.

There are a number of generalist databases available, including *Google Scholar*, *Scopus* and *Web of Science*. These are multidisciplinary scholarly databases with broad, international coverage and a focus on academic literature rather than websites. There are also a number of databases that will be particularly relevant to your own discipline. For example, *ERIC* (Educational Resources Information Center) is an important database for education; *PsycINFO* is a main database for psychology, *Historical Abstracts* is the primary source for world history (excluding the United States and Canada) from the 15th century; *AnthroSource* searches across the journals published by the American Anthropological Association; *Business Source Complete* represents a business database; and *Sociological Abstracts* contains scholarly international coverage of sociology, social sciences, economics and women's studies. You will be able to search the relevant reference databases for sources of information.

A number of other indexes focus on citations and are likely to be available through your university library. These databases include the *Social Sciences Citations Index*, the *Arts & Humanities Citation Index* and the *Science Citation Index*. They allow you to track who has cited a particular article and where and when it was cited. Typically, you will enter into the database search engine a reference to a seminal study in your topic area. The citation index will then provide you with information on the author, source and publication date of all the scholarly work that has cited the initial article. The advantage of the citation index is that it provides you with a whole collection of very recent (and not so recent) work specific to your topic area. A search through a citation index will, like a search through a reference database, yield the abstract of the article. It will also provide you with access to the full text of the article if your university has subscribed to the journal in question.

How do we get the best outcome from searching through databases? Searching can, after all, be very time-consuming. Sometimes it can also be downright frustrating. The approach is to use keywords and define boundaries, and the good news is that you have already successfully defined your key concepts and set boundaries around your research. Let's stop for a moment to look at Bill's research, which we explored in Chapter 2 (Case Study 2.2). Bill had chosen to explore the ways in which one effective teacher develops a community of learners in a grade 12 mathematics classroom, and had decided to theorize the research through 'communities of practice'. Putting boundaries around his research led him to identify 'mathematics', 'grade 12' and 'middle set'. From his conceptual framework he had already done the hard initial work for his search.

Bill hoped to run a search engine using the parameters and key words he had identified. But first he needed to come up with a few alternatives (synonyms) for his key words. Knowing that he might need to modify his synonyms as a result of his search, he came up with the following:

mathematics: numeracy; calculus; algebra; statistics; geometry
grade 12:   year 12; 16-17 years of age; upper secondary school;
                    upper high school; higher level students
middle set: middle band; middle stream
effective teaching: quality teaching; best practice

Now Bill is ready to explore the database. He knows that if he carried out single searches for all his key words the information he found would be so extensive it would probably be unmanageable. Instead he uses a facility known as Boolean Operators and a technique known as truncation to obtain the most relevant information from his search.

Bill restricts the number of results by using the Boolean Operators 'AND', 'OR' and 'NOT'. He searches for 'mathematics AND grade 12 OR middle set' to indicate that he is looking for sources that explore mathematics along with either grade 12 or middle set. Because he does not wish to search for sources that refer to primary school he could have used 'mathematics NOT primary school mathematics'.

As Bill was working through the process it occurrs to him that his intentions would not necessarily be captured if he just focuses on 'mathematics'. He is aware that words such as 'maths' or 'math' are often used in place of 'mathematics'. Using the truncation feature he identifies the part that the words have in common (math) and follows the letters with an asterisk (*), which is the conventional symbol to indicate other endings would be acceptable. A search using 'math*' captures the terms 'mathematics', 'maths', 'math', 'mathematizing', 'mathematical', and a number of similar words beginning with 'math'. Bill's strategy may need to be repeated using either refined or broadened search terms. It may mean identifying a time span for the publication of sources. Searching through databases is almost always a trial-and-error process, invariably yielding material that is excessive or limited in scope.

Activity

DATABASE SEARCHING

From your conceptual framework:

1. Write out your key words or key phrases.
2. Make a list of synonyms (words with similar meaning) for each of your key words.
3. Combine the synonyms for each concept with OR.
4. Combine your concepts with AND.
5. Add together the OR combinations and the AND combinations.

Logging your references

Searching through databases is an important skill in which you will become proficient. A second skill will be learning how to log and manage all those references that made it to the relevant pile. Finding out about bibliographic software packages, and how to make best use of them for your work is a real must. Software tools for storing and managing your references include ProCite, EndNote, RefWorks and Reference Manager. They are tools by which you can create your own reference database. Think about the software as a contemporary and more sophisticated version of the card record-keeping system. As a research student you may find that you qualify for a paid licence for one of these bibliographic management packages. If not, then similar but simplified packages are available at no expense from the internet.

But what will the advantages be? They are too numerous to name. To give a few examples, bibliographic management packages provide you with a systematic record-keeping structure to log your references, either directly from your library catalogue or manually. Bibliographic software packages also allow you to manage your references, to group them by theme, time period and so on at the click of a button. They allow you to cite while you write, producing an ordered and accurate reference list at the end of the piece which is formatted in the citation style of your choice. But that is not all bibliographic software packages do; they also record the abstract and provide you with the means to import the full text of the article you are referencing. They also allow you to personalize the database by providing you with a number of fields for your own entries.

In short, bibliographic management packages allow you to:

- import and store references from library catalogues and electronic databases;
- sort and search your references;
- download and manage full texts;
- create bibliographies immediately in a variety of bibliographic styles; and
- insert citations into your documents.

Many postgraduate researchers have said that time spent learning how to use a bibliographic package is time well spent that will save you hours and hours of work later on. My advice is to make a one-to-one appointment with the librarian responsible for your discipline at your university. Ask for a hands-on lesson using a bibliographic package early in your study, and take time to practise your skills at your own computer. At a future time, when you need further library assistance, you will be able to contact this librarian directly.

Of course it will often not be realistic for you to log all the references from your database search. You need to carry out an initial screening to discard any articles that are not directly relevant to your topic. To carry out that screening simply skim read through the abstracts of each article, identifying those that are not relevant, those that are marginally relevant and those that are relevant. You might consider using a 'traffic light' coding system of relevance in which red is for 'discard', amber is for 'has potential', and green is for 'relevant'. Once coded, enter all the references that made into the 'relevant' pile into your personal bibliographic system.

Critiquing your references

One of the fundamental skills of a researcher is critique. You will need to develop the skill of evaluating other people's work, and that means not taking the article at face value. In the research that you finally produce you need to demonstrate not only a command and appreciation of the intellectual significance of your topic but also your critical evaluation in terms of the strengths and limitations of the existing body of knowledge. Reading, reflecting on and evaluating the literature in your subject area are critical stages in the planning of your research. At this stage you are beginning to know quite a lot about research problems and research questions. While you may not yet fully appreciate issues surrounding the methodology, you will at least be able to assess whether the design of the study is appropriate for finding answers to the research question. On the basis of your critical evaluation, you might decide to eliminate some literature sources. Alternatively, you might decide to use your critique of a particular source as a means of strengthening the rationale for your own study. You must be able to defend your position if you do not agree with the perspective presented in a particular source.

Many postgraduate researchers are concerned about their role as an evaluator of other people's work. Critiquing experienced researchers' work is sometimes perceived to be an inappropriate activity for newcomers.

INSIGHTS FROM A POSTGRADUATE RESEARCHER

"At this stage of my research, I know I need to improve my critical analysis skills and this is actually the main reason for me doing research. Self-doubt creeps in, you think your views don't matter because you are just a beginner, and that you are trying to critique the work of experts in their fields who are established, published authors. The other problem is that I keep measuring ideas and research against my own 'yardstick' of experience in secondary school teaching. This would work in a classroom, that wouldn't, teachers wouldn't use that. It's too theoretical and divorced from the realities of the classroom because teachers literally often teach minute by minute. And on it goes…"

Keep in mind that being critical does not mean criticizing or being negative. In research, adopting a critical stance means analyzing carefully and making an informed assessment. We can explain it more deeply. Being critical begins with respect for the authors, open-mindedness and taking a constructive position. It involves questioning and scrutiny of the claims authors make. It requires examining the consistency of their claims and whether or not those claims are substantiated by the evidence provided.

Reading your literature sources from a critical standpoint will always be undertaken in relation to the focus of your own research and what you already know about your topic area. Basically, you want to determine whether the source under investigation is leading edge, old hat, logically consistent, credible, flawed or exemplary.

Case Study 3.2

JACQUI'S RESEARCH

Exploring effective professional development for on-line tertiary instructors

CRITIQUING THE LITERATURE

Jacqui had read numerous literature sources relating to her topic. She was particularly interested in a journal article written by three key authors working in the area of professional learning for on-line tertiary teachers. She wanted to know if the findings of the study undertaken by these experienced authors might be relevant in her own context. She applied a critical lens to the task of reading the article and noted down the following as she read:

- aim, methods and findings clearly outlined
- a wider range of international studies would better contextualize the study
- research questions are identified but could be more clearly stated
- the method aligns with the aims of the study
- a surprisingly high response rate to participation
- inducements to participation are recorded; how trustworthy are the findings?
- very descriptive report; where are the explanations?
- no attempt is made to acknowledge any limitations of applying the findings to other settings

---

Like Jacqui you can put on your researcher's critical hat to evaluate literature relevant to your topic. And like Jacqui, you might also find that experienced authors' work does not stand up to inspection. The Set of Helpful Criteria for Assessing Research outlines a framework that you might use to guide you in your evaluations. The criteria are grouped under headings raising the following questions:

- What was the purpose?
- Who was it written for?
- What questions were being asked?
- What answers were found and what conclusions were drawn?
- Where is the evidence?

At a fundamental level the headings are asking you to consider:

- What have I learned from my critique and how will I be able to use the article in my own work?

As you become more and more familiar with what to look for in your critique of literature sources you will become faster and more skilled at

A SET OF HELPFUL CRITERIA FOR ASSESSING RESEARCH

Purpose	Are the aims of the research clear?
Justification	Is the rationale for the study clear?
	What is the significance of the research?
	What are its implications?
Prior Research	Has the relevant literature been examined and summarized?
	Have all the issues which impinge on the topic been considered?
	Is there 'a gap' in the literature which is addressed in this research?
Problem and Questions	Is the research problem clearly identified?
	Are the research questions clear and answerable?
Research Design	Is the design clearly outlined and appropriate?
	Will it provide an answer to the research questions?
	Are instrument construction and sampling clear?
	Is data analysis clear and appropriate?
	Are validity and reliability considered?
	Are limitations acknowledged?
	Are ethical issues addressed?
Interpretation of findings	Is the written description of the findings consistent with the data?
	Are the interpretations consistent with the findings?
	Are the research questions answered?

Activity

CRITIQUING A LITERATURE SOURCE

1. Choose an article relevant to your topic.
2. Using the Set of Helpful Criteria, draw up a table to assess the problem, research design, research method or approach, methods of data collection and analysis, as well as results and findings of the article.
3. Write a sentence describing how the systematic evaluation matched your original assessment of the article.

making your critical evaluations. A systematic process will help you to avoid repetition of work and prevent you from wasting your precious time. Before long, you will be proficient at entering your evaluations directly into your bibliographic record of the articles. Essentially, the process involves organizing your citations while, simultaneously, constructing the foundation for the literature review ahead. That is the endpoint we are seeking.

At this stage you have entries in your bibliographic package, along with an attachment in portable document format (pdf) of the article or report. Now you are in a strong position to write a summary paragraph on how the reference fits with your research, along with a short assessment of the source. It will be very useful if you add into the Notes field any quotations (and page numbers) that you consider might be useful within the literature review that you will be writing during the next stage. These summary paragraphs and the quotations (that may later be paraphrased or used directly as quotations) will form the backbone of the review ahead.

Review

Main points

- The literature assists you in understanding your topic and research problem more acutely.
- In examining the literature more deeply and widely, you will become more informed of what is happening in your topic area.
- The literature influences the specific direction your research will take.
- A key purpose of the literature is to contexualize your own research.
- The literature will provide an indication of how you might contribute to the debate around your topic.
- A wide range of sources provides information for your research.
- Much of the information can be found through reference databases.
- Search strategies are used for retrieving information.
- Bilbilographic software packages help in the organization of literature sources.
- Critique is an important skill to develop.

Key Terms

- Literature sources
- Literature searches
- Bibliographic management systems
- Literature critique

Looking ahead

In the next chapter the literature sources, and a critique of them, are used as a starting point for constructing the literature review. The chapter considers how to synthesize the sources already assembled. It explores how to construct an academic argument that is coherent and directly relevant to your topic. It also examines the challenges of writing and explores the conventions associated with a literature review.

4 Writing the Literature Review

The necessity of the literature review

The literature plays a significant role in your research. Without a body of literature your own research would be undertaken in a vacuum and you would be unable to engage in the discussions and debates that are moving thinking forward in your area. Since you hope to demonstrate that you want to be part of these important discussions, you will need to show that you are conversant with the work that engages other researchers in your area. You will need to identify the seminal studies. You will also need to demonstrate that you have a clear understanding of the key issues and controversies, and that you have a handle on cutting-edge developments specific to your area. Anchoring your study in the context of relevant previous research will ensure that you are not charged with unfamiliarity of the field.

An analogy here might assist. Suppose you are invited to a drinks party. When you arrive at the venue, lively conversations are already taking place. You gravitate towards a group of people. As a newcomer to the group you listen carefully to what is being said before intruding, and when the moment seems right you make a small contribution to the discussion. Research is rather like the drinks conversation involving a number of people interested in a topic. Some participants will share similar views and others will have alternative perceptions on the topic. As a new researcher you 'listen' to what is being debated. You do that through accessing, assessing and assembling literature sources, making decisions about what will be useful to your own work and what should be excluded. Then you demonstrate to others through the literature review that you are aware of the current debates and argue the case for your own contribution to the discussions. Your research will always be in relation to what others have said, both within and beyond the discipline of your topic.

Briefly then, the literature review situates your proposed study in relation to the existing body of knowledge. It is a requirement in research projects, dissertations and theses. The thing to appreciate here is that the literature review will allow you to build a case for conducting your study. It will inform the design and data collection, as well as the analysis of your results. On completion of your study you will return to the literature review to establish the specific contribution your work makes to the field.

You could think of the literature review as an intelligence-gathering activity. It is, in effect, its own separate research project. In researching literature sources, you are probing your area of research interest from all perspectives with a bird's eye view. Rather than coming up with something completely new, or already knowing the right answers, through a balanced account of the literature you are trying to demonstrate that you are in command of what has been written on and around your topic. An important fact to remember is that good research is judged in relation to a particular existing and up-to-date body of knowledge. Showing that you know the work of your professional community, and are aware of the kind of contribution you will make with your research, will hold you in good stead.

Case Study 4.1

LOOKING AT LITERATURE SOURCES FOR MICHAEL'S TOPIC

Michael was interested in studying workplace conversations within a shoe factory. He sourced literature on general workplace talk and more specific literature related to talk within the manufacturing enterprise. His investigation extended to studies exploring workers' and supervisors' types of talk. His literature search included reports of studies on talk amongst shift workers at different times of the day. Michael also gathered sources on dialogue patterns within small groups and within two-person interactions, and on studies that reported on interactions between workers and supervisors.

The literature review is a pathway for you to become an expert in the field. There is simply no escaping from the writing (McMillan and Weyers, 2013). You may, understandably, feel daunted by the prospect of putting your writing skills on display. Putting things in perspective: to reach this stage in your student life, you have already demonstrated your competency at writing. Take a moment to reflect on the number of assignments and essays you wrote as an undergraduate (and possibly graduate) student in which you communicated ideas in an academic way. You have already jumped through the first writing hoops and, with some guidance, you will be able to tackle the task and produce a fine literature review.

INSIGHTS FROM A POSTGRADUATE RESEARCHER

"I remember how overwhelmed I felt with the thought of doing the literature review. I would sit at my desk, fixed on the blank page on the computer screen, completely out of my comfort zone. I almost wished a fairy godmother would come along and tap out the review for me. To be honest, I didn't know how to begin. I thought that finding more and more literature would solve the problem and the penny would finally drop, but of course it didn't. Even my supervisor couldn't offer any helpful advice. And the more I procrastinated the closer the deadline for the first draft of the review approached."

Maximizing the positive aspects of your writing

There are a few techniques that might assist you in writing the literature review (Craswell, 2005). It is important to schedule in regular time for writing and setting manageable goals and realistic deadlines for a piece of writing (Castello, Inesta and Monereo, 2009). Take care over what other activities you commit to while working on your research. Remember that getting under way with your literature review should remain your overriding concern at the moment, and more important than any 'displacement activities' in which you might be tempted to become involved.

In considering your workspace, ask yourself:

- Do you prefer an environment where you can see and hear others rather than be hidden away in a distraction-free workspace?
- Do you work best when you can tick off daily writing tasks on a to-do list? Small rewards for completion of a small piece of work are important.

Now consider how you begin a new writing task:

- Do you like to jot down a few ideas, key words or phrases and then work them together in a way that ignores all the rules of academic prose before you attend to protocols of prose writing?
- Do you like to focus on grammar, sentence and paragraph structure right from the start?

Once you understand your approach and focus on creating arrangements and conditions that will be conducive to your writing, your confidence in your own writing abilities will develop.

There are a number of avenues you can explore to get some clues about what is expected of you, and what a good literature review looks like. You can check out exemplary examples of scholarly reviews published in journals or handbooks that are dedicated to reviewing the literature. If you are not able to identify these sources at this stage, you could ask your supervisor or advisor for the names of them. You might choose to look at past theses or research reports to learn how others have approached the writing process. You might also want to check out the support your university offers in addition to your supervision arrangements. Many universities have structures in place that provide writing support. Take advantage of these.

Informal writing support groups sometimes develop amongst postgraduate researchers enrolled on the same course. Talking through any research problems with a support group can often open up possible solutions to writing difficulties. Remember, however, that if you seek feedback and support from other postgraduate researchers, you must also be prepared to give constructive feedback to those postgraduate researchers.

INSIGHTS FROM A POSTGRADUATE RESEARCHER

"We had heard about support groups and wanted to try it out ourselves. Because we are all busy people we decided to meet up early in the day on a regular basis. And that's how our breakfast club was formed. We meet every fortnight at 7.30 am at the same café. Sometimes we share our problems with our work and sometimes we just talk about other things. It's really good to know that there is always someone who will listen. Last week I was stuck on the getting the right tone in my literature review and the girls in the breakfast club gave me a few suggestions."

You might use the group to test out a few writing ideas, or you might want to receive feedback on a small piece of writing. Some writing groups will expect you to read the piece of writing in question. Difficult though this might be at first, it is an excellent way of highlighting problems to do with listener engagement, grammar, syntax, tone, repetitiveness, sentence length, monotony and the like. It is also a way of establishing whether your writing flows in a logically organized and confident manner. Ask yourself whether there was a sense of coherence between the ideas presented within the piece. You might want to consider reading sections out loud to yourself in the comfort of your own workspace to check these details.

As any postgraduate researcher knows, there are days when the writing simply skips along by itself. There are other days when inspiration escapes you entirely and nothing much seems to come together. Here is a suggestion for those 'other days': as you complete a writing session, write a note setting out a small and realistic objective for when you come back to writing. On return, check over what you wrote last session, remind yourself of your objective for this session and spend a short time weighing up approaches that might achieve that objective. If the writing is still not forthcoming, then choose another activity related to your research, such as organizing your literature sources or checking references. At all costs, avoid wasting your precious study time on unrelated tasks.

Creating a structure for the literature review

If you want to produce your most polished effort and if you want to learn from the writing, you need to write as you go. The writing is guaranteed to take a lot longer than you anticipate. It involves lots of drafts and revising, and, what's more, it continues to evolve throughout the research process. Like it or not, the important point to emphasize is that you will add to the literature review throughout the course of your research. You will need the persistence of a sniffer dog on the literature trail right through to the end. In actual fact, there is never an end to a literature review. But for the purposes of your project, the endpoint will be drawn when you submit your report or thesis of your research.

It is vitally important to put your first thoughts in writing as soon as possible. Many postgraduate researchers speak of the writing stage as a period of time they allocate to the task for later on in the research process. Procrastinating over your writing is far from ideal. Getting started will not be so difficult if you build on the summaries and quotations you wrote in your database. There isn't any magic to writing the literature review, just things to learn.

In the preceding chapter we explored avenues for accessing and managing the literature. We developed a systematic record-keeping system: when you accessed a literature source you read through the Abstract and made a decision about whether or not to include the reference within your literature review. Those literature sources that made it into the inclusion pile were subsequently entered, along with a pdf of the document into the software tool (such as EndNote, ProCite, RefWorks, or Reference Manager) which you are using to manage your bibliography. You then wrote a summary paragraph on how the source fitted with your research. You also added into the Notes field any quotations (and page numbers) that you considered might be useful within your review. Now it is time to benefit from the notes you made on individual literature sources. In essence, while you were organizing your citations and building your personal library, you were also constructing the foundation for your literature review.

The summary paragraphs and the quotations (that may later be paraphrased or used directly as quotations) will form the backbone of the review. Consider how you might organize the ideas you have collected. Will they be best organised through themes? Through time periods? There are other possibilities, such as structuring the discussion according to local or international research, or different theoretical and methodological approaches. Suppose you settle on a thematic approach to your literature review. First, list all the themes and/or variables that have emerged. The themes will become your headings within your literature review. Of course you may later wish to delete or add a theme, or combine two or more themes, but at this early stage you have the foundation for your review.

The headings and sub-headings you construct within your literature review will shine light on what is in store for the reader. It will be necessary to use section headings to break up the extensive content of the literature review for ease of reading and for introducing new themes. The written headings you choose will act like mini–reviews to organize the literature base. In addition to the written headings, postgraduate researchers often use numbering systems to differentiate between the themes in the content matter. Obviously there needs to be clear links between similar parts of a numbering system. While divisions are often necessary within the literature review it is important to keep in mind that too many layers of headings tend to create a lack of cohesion.

In Case Study 4.2, Vanessa is planning a self-study (Casey, 2012) of her teaching of socio-scientific issues and ethical decision-making to senior secondary school students. She has begun a first draft of the structure of her literature review, using the themes that emerged from her database of literature sources.

Case Study 4.2

TOPIC: TEACHING CRITICAL LITERACY SKILLS AND ETHICAL DECISION-MAKING AT THE TERTIARY LEVEL: A SELF-STUDY

STUDENT: Vanessa

CHAPTER 2 DRAFT LITERATURE REVIEW

2.1. Introduction

2.2. Self-Study

    2.2.1. Reflective Practice

    2.2.2. Autoethnography

    2.2.3. Action Research

    2.2.4. Student Voice

    2.2.5. Journalling

    2.2.6. Critical Incidents

    2.2.7. Self-Study in Practice

2.3. Critical Literacy Issues

    2.3.1. Critical Literacy at the Tertiary Level in the United Kingdom

    2.3.2. Teaching Critical Literacy in the United Kingdom

    2.3.3. Students' Perspectives of Critical Literacy Teaching

2.4. Ethical Inquiry

2.5. Quality Teaching

2.6. Summary

Vanessa took some time over developing the structure of the literature review. Once she had identified the items for inclusion in the review, she asked her support group to help her talk through the relationships between each source. She found it easier to put her ideas on a large piece of paper and draw connecting lines between sources to illustrate major and minor relationships. After much discussion and crossing-out, as well as additions of lines, she produced a draft structure on her office wall. As she got into her writing she found that the basic structure helped her to organize her writing and allowed her to keep hold of the review's big picture. However, the draft structure was not exactly what she finally presented. As a case in point, she found as she began to write that she could create a stronger argument by separating the sub-sub-sections 2.2.4, 2.2.5, and 2.2.6 from sub-section 2.2 and forming a new sub-section. Her final structure gave her a sense of immense accomplishment.

The process for Bill, whom we met in Chapter 2, was much simpler. Earlier, in developing a conceptual framework for this study, Bill was also making hard decisions about what to include in the literature review. His research was focused on exploring the ways in which one effective teacher develops a community of learners in a grade 12 mathematics classroom. Through his conceptual framework he had also figured out what themes might be important to discuss in the review and what order he might discuss them. Directly from his conceptual framework he drafted the headings for his review as in Case Study 4.3.

Since this was Bill's first attempt at an organization for his literature review he remained open-minded about the possibility of change. He suspected that he might need to combine or add to some of the 2.4 sub-sections but chose to wait to see how his thinking developed as a result of writing the review. As he read more and began to write he realized that sub-sub-section 2.4.4 'Responding to students' might need to become a new sub-section to align with his focus on developing a community of learners. One point to emphasize here relates to the order of subheadings. The structure of Bill's literature review seems to suggest that he will work through the writing systematically from beginning to end. In fact very few postgraduate researchers work in a sequential fashion. Many postgraduate researchers like to begin with a section that they know will be relatively straightforward, and possibly relatively short, and then deal with the potentially more difficult and longer sections later.

Don't get it right, get it written

In the last chapter we explored ways to assess a literature source and you will have recorded on your bibliographic database all the sources that might end up in your literature review. Postgraduate researchers sometimes think

---

Case Study 4.3

TOPIC: THE EFFECTIVE DEVELOPMENT OF A COMMUNITY OF
LEARNERS: A CASE STUDY

STUDENT: Bill

CHAPTER 2 DRAFT LITERATURE REVIEW

2.1. Introduction

2.2. Official Policies

    2.2.1. National Curriculum Statements on Teaching And Learning

    2.2.2. School Policies on Teaching and Learning – Principal/School Board

    2.2.3. Maths Department Policies on Teaching And Learning

2.3. Teacher Characteristics

    2.3.1. Teaching Experiences

    2.3.2. Qualifications

    2.3.3. Views of Teaching and Learning

    2.3.4. Professional Learning Experiences

2.4. Classroom Features

    2.4.1. Planning

    2.4.2. Instructing

    2.4.3. Selecting Tasks and Activities

    2.4.4. Responding to Students

    2.4.5. Questioning

    2.4.6. Using Hands-on Equipment and Technology

    2.4.7. Assessing Understanding

2.5. Student Outcomes

    2.5.1. Academic Achievements

    2.5.2. Social and Behavioural Outcomes

2.6. Summary

---

that they need to cite every single piece of relevant work, even if some are related only in a tangential way to the study. My advice is to be selective. Keep in mind that the literature review in its entirety should reveal to the reader that your reading is relevant and well-chosen to align with your own work, and it should demonstrate that you are capable of adding a contribution to this body of work. It needs to be up to date. However, you should consider including classic work that is important to your area, but bear in mind that most work from 15 to 20 years ago never reached 'classic' status.

Depending on your discipline and your topic, your literature review is likely to be weighted more heavily towards some kinds of sources than others. For example, you might discuss primary sources predominantly and use secondary sources only when primary sources are not available or accessible. Or, your literature sources might largely comprise secondary sources. You will need to discuss what is appropriate with your supervisor. Again, depending on the discipline, practitioner-oriented literature might be used to support the points you wish to make. An important guide as to numbers of sources will be the requirements of the qualification you are seeking. Generally speaking, a research project may require engagement with 20 or so of the most relevant and recent journal articles. On the other hand, a doctoral qualification will demand a very much larger number of literature sources of recent and not-so-recent work, and will include theoretical papers.

In your literature database you will have recorded your evaluation of each source. These will be particularly important for the writing of the review since you will be attempting to write beyond the level of description. This means that in the review, by themselves, quotations from publications will not be sufficient. Your review will offer an argued explanation of the topic, including the strengths and weaknesses of the previous studies you have found. It will identify any inconsistencies amongst those studies. It will set boundaries and will locate gaps that will point to the need for your study. That is to say, it will clarify how the existing knowledge base might be developed further and how thinking might be extended by your own proposed investigation. In a sense you are using the literature review as a way of mapping out your claim to a particular territory.

One way to map out your claim to a territory is to think of the literature review as a story built around a plot. The argument you want to express represents the plot. Anything that is relevant to the argument will need to be expressed coherently with respect to that plot. In other words, you will need to show how those aspects fit into the larger argument that you are presenting. Indeed, the hallmark of scholarly research reporting is an argument that is sufficiently convincing to represent a contribution to new knowledge within your field of study. In scholarly terms, when you present an argument within your literature review, you are creating a discussion around information and a series of claims relating to that information. You

---

INSIGHTS FROM A POSTGRADUATE RESEARCHER

"I had more than 30 sources to incorporate into my literature review. I kept telling myself that we were not expected to just summarize. We had to build the literature review into a 'story' with themes and to have our own 'voice' evident in the way we critiqued the literature. But I enjoy writing, especially crafting those linking paragraphs and transitions, so that part wasn't really a problem for me. Nor was the gathering of those sources of information, writing research notes and looking for links and themes. (I am a dedicated patterns and themes hunter)."

substantiate those claims with compelling evidence from literature sources and draw the threads of the discussion together by noting the significance of your point of view.

The important point is that you are not simply reproducing the views of others. You are demonstrating that you have made an interpretation and evaluation of relevant work to support your own argument. Think about the review in terms of trying to persuade the reader to align their view of a problem or issue with yours. However, as we know from everyday life, people are not always easily persuaded. Research readers are possibly even more sceptical. Persuasive arguments establish credibility by offering clarity and, more specifically, by providing a chain of reasoning for the reader that is logical and that leads towards acceptance of the points being made.

INSIGHTS FROM A POSTGRADUATE RESEARCHER

"Writing the literature review with a critical eye was a challenging job. In fact the key skill I really needed for my literature review was critical analysis."

The way you present an argument will *not* resemble a series of disconnected commentaries or, worse, 'he said/she said' discussions. Undeniably, creating an argument is difficult work (Fink, 2005). Many literature reviews walk the reader through a succession of interesting ideas *without* making connections. Be careful not to produce a literature review of that kind. Remember to make it easier for the reader by building up the central argument. Guide the reader by signposting. Have an informed view of what your reader would know already. If your work is highly novel, then you will need to be sure that your themes are presented in an introductory way.

You will then need to make a case for the importance of your chosen themes in ways that the audience can readily recognize. Connect them to the debates taking place. Since you cannot expect that every reader will be sympathetic to the argument you put forward, it is important that you provide sound support from the literature. Rather than positioning your research on the fringe of debate in your chosen topic area, you need to locate it centrally, linked to current arguments. Making your research explicitly central to the debate allows you to clarify your use of terms and expressions in comparison with the ways in which these have been used in other work in your targeted field. For example, in Michael's example (Case Study 3.3), the concept of 'talk' was fundamental to his work. He will need to show how his use of the term is distinguished from other usages of the term in the literature.

Be cautious about presenting too many peripheral ideas that run counter to your central argument. Take care to avoid sentences of a huge significance and moment before the reader is ready for them. Pacing is important.

Refrain from giving away too much too early. On the other hand, don't be too slow in bringing your central argument to the surface of the discussion. Be explicit about the sequencing of various elements within your literature review, clarifying how each, progressively, supports your argument, so that the reader feels in command of the sequence of the thoughts expressed. If you can do that, all the various threads will be pulled together in order to create a seamless story.

Communicating with your reader

First impressions are extremely important to the reader. Many readers are able to conjure up their views of the quality of a literature review very quickly. As they journey through your writing they will expect to be able to navigate with the help of a roadmap and clear signposts. One easy way to offer signposting is by introducing the literature review with an overview of the chapter and its structure. Clarification like this might seem obvious but it is surprising how many postgraduate researchers choose to plunge their readers directly in at the deep end. There are a number of other stepping stones that you can offer your reader.

- Acknowledge all your sources.
- Make sure that your formatting is consistent.
- Be consistent in your use of specific terminology. Readers will expect this, and don't want to experience confusion.
- You may decide to delete specific words from your chapter. You will particularly want to prune out qualifiers (e.g., 'sort of', 'quite', 'very') and value words (e.g., 'bad', 'disastrous'), as well as strings of adjectives.
- You may decide to delete a sentence, a paragraph or even a section from your chapter. Keep these deletions in another file just in case you decide to use them later.

When you feel you have done your best to engage the reader at the chapter level, leave it for a while. When you return to it you will read it with fresh eyes.

What you are really trying to do through your literature review is communicate clearly with your reader. You want to make a case for your proposed study, and make it clear to your reader that you know what has already been found on the topic. Individual sentences and clusters of sentences are the key mechanism by which you build communication with your reader and engagement with your argument. How many scholarly pieces have you read that are extraordinarily difficult to wade through? The difficulty could well be the result of the writer expressing too many ideas within a paragraph. If that is the case, it is likely that the sentences are long and rambling. Conciseness and simplicity are important. Just as readers do not appreciate overly-long and complex sentences, they also do not appreciate sentences that are too brusque. Variation in sentence length is what they most welcome and is what will help cultivate their interest.

Crafting a clear argument will not be possible without paying attention to the functions and conventions of paragraphs. The function of a paragraph is to create a deliberate break or pause for the reader to signal that you are introducing a new discussion into a section. You may take several paragraphs to complete the full discussion of your argument, at which point you will draw all the discussion threads together for the reader. Paragraphs related to a specific point must be presented in a logical order. The overarching message or the point you want to convey to the reader is written up and known as the topic sentence. The topic sentence of a paragraph presents only one key message, and that message should be succinct and clearly expressed, avoid unnecessary jargon, and be easily grasped by your reader. Avoid saying too much in your paragraph. Once you offer the reader more than one topic sentence, the text becomes confusing. If a new idea warrants its own discussion, you should shift it to form a new paragraph. Otherwise delete it. Often, but not always, the topic sentence that outlines the point you wish to make will be placed near the beginning or the end of the paragraph. All the other sentences within the paragraph will have a logical connection with the key idea expressed in your topic sentence. Some of the supporting sentences will complement your key idea. Other sentences will set out the relevance of your argument.

We will apply the rules of paragraph writing to the presentation of the argument you wish to make in your literature review. When developing your main argument you are likely to need several paragraphs, perhaps even sections, to get your point across. You need to provide evidence from authoritative sources within the literature or concrete or practical examples from other relevant sources to substantiate your argument and, as well, to offer counter-examples to set up a contradiction which you will then refute. To create your own argument you could use a combination of direct quotes and paraphrasing. Do not assume that the reader is already aware of all the points you wish to make. Your points need to be spelt out carefully in a process akin to guided discovery. Take the reader slowly along with you. Do not put in too much of significance or too many fundamentals before the reader is ready for them. Rather than giving away too much too early you should build your argument up slowly.

Along the way you will offer supporting sentences that emphasize and complement your argument more strongly or that contradict your view. Sentences need to make clear sense. Be sure that the subject and verb of the sentence are placed closely together. Many postgraduate researchers fall into the habit of starting a new sentence with 'this', such as in 'This created a problem...' or 'This meant that....' As a result, the reader is often left wondering what 'this' refers to. Clarify the antecedent. Good writing makes explicit who is doing what. Good writing also uses transitions between sentences. Smooth transitions are equally important between paragraphs. Clear transitional sentences or words such as 'additionally', 'subsequently' and 'on the other hand' are crucially important in the construction of an argument.

What you particularly want to avoid is a situation in which readers feel they are being led through a disconnected succession of ideas. The literature review needs to be coherent. That is to say, the thread of your argument needs to run through the literature review. Readers should always be clear how one section leads to another. You will need to be explicit about how each piece of evidence progressively supports (or does not support) your argument. Be clear about whether or not you are aligning yourself with the various views. Is the evidence from others obviously right, obviously wrong, or just in line with your preferences? On what basis has the evidence been selected? Is it because it marks out the same territory as you? Parading fragments of the work of various authors will only be fruitful if you can clarify whether or not you agree with that work and identify the extent to which those references pinpoint your own position. Be upfront in asserting your reasons for your position. Weaving your argument into the discussion and sequencing the examples carefully will be vital for helping readers feel they are in command of your thinking. Developing a logical sequence of moves and stages will help you develop a sharper argument that is responsive to your reader. The supporting sequences will then lead to an establishment of the relevance of the point you are making with your overall argument.

Since you are not yet considered an expert in the field, take care over the tone in which you present your argument. At the same time, you don't want to appear too deferential. You will need to maintain a humble-yet-confident register consistently throughout. But making a persuasive case involves more than tone. It involves writing a narrative that will capture the imagination of the reader, responding to an anticipated level of critique. In capturing the imagination of your reader the successful writer marshals sound reasoning and, in the process, turns complex ideas into elegant and easily accessible arguments.

Complying with conventions

There are always rules to follow in any form of communication. Look at the example of e-communication. There is an established set of protocols around sending and receiving emails. For example, as a sender, you are required to minimize writing in capitals, to write a topic in the subject line, to typically begin your salutation in a less formal manner than in printed communication, and so forth. Since other senders of emails tend to follow the same set of protocols, communication becomes unproblematic. When

CRITIQUING MY DRAFT LITERATURE REVIEW

Read through your draft literature review

1. Is your central argument clear to a reader?
2. Have you supported the case you want to make with sources from the literature?
3. Check that you delivered what you promised in your introduction.
4. Check that you conclude the review with a short summary of the ideas presented.
5. Read the paragraphs in a section carefully. Is there one topic sentence in each paragraph?
6. Are all the sentences within each paragraph closely related to the topic sentence?
7. Have you used complex terminology when simple words would suffice?
8. Are the transitions between sentences and between paragraphs smooth?

a writer of the literature review follows the protocols that a reader expects, then communication is also fairly easy.

Your readers will expect you to communicate in a particular way. They will appreciate a number of technical aspects such as reasonably wide margins, double spacing and consistent font and type size. They will be expecting you to apply standard grammatical rules, using an academic genre, so you need to avoid clichés, jargon, abbreviated forms of words such as 'won't', expletives and offensive language. They will anticipate that your quotations support rather than establish or summarize a point you want to make, and will expect to see appropriate attribution given for those quotations. They will assume that you have read and will cite original sources, even though you may also have looked at secondary sources as a way into the literature. Depending on the discipline, they may accept the use of 'I' but would not react so favourably to the use of 'we' and 'us'.

Readers will expect to see references presented in the conventional form for the discipline (Pears and Shields, 2008). Every time you cite another work you will need to be sure that you provide a reference, both in the text and in the reference list at the end. The References list all (but only those) references that were included in your literature review. It includes all works to which you refer in the in-text citations, and, if used, the footnotes and the endnotes. You should not list sources in the reference list that you have not drawn on in your work. The reference list is an acknowledgement of the sources that you have found sufficiently useful to include in your review. It also makes it possible for others to follow up on those documents. Since the entries in the reference list form part of the evidence to support your argument, information gained from other sources without due acknowledgement may be read as plagiarized material. Hence it is vitally important that you pay referencing its due respect.

Many postgraduate researchers use the American Psychological Association (APA) referencing style and this is the one we will look at briefly here. However, there are a number of referencing styles and since some disciplines do not use APA, you will need to familiarize yourself with the specific referencing style demanded by your discipline.

If the bibliographic database you are using includes a facility that allows you to cite while you write, then you might want to skip the following section and focus your attention on learning how to use the citation tool. If not, then learn APA style by using it.

Common in-text citations

When you cite specific work within the body of the text, the convention is to record the author's name and the year of the publication in a way that does not interrupt the flow of your argument. One of two approaches will be appropriate in each situation.

1. (i) Maple (2014) argues that regular gardening activity is associated with health.
   (ii) Elm and Oak (2015) have argued for connections between gardening activity and health.
2. (i) Associations between regular gardening activity and health have been identified (Elm, 2014; Maple, 2015; Oak, 2013).
   (ii) Gardening activity and health are related (Maple, Sycamore, & Conifer, 2015; Prunus & Magnolia, 2014).

Notice that it is the alphabetical order of authors rather than the order of publication year that prevails. Notice, too, when to use '&' and when to use 'and' (and that this book does not use APA conventions for '&' and 'and'). Be sure that you list the authors in exactly the same way as they are given in the original document.

Quotations of fewer than 40 words 'run-on' in the text. You will need to use double quotation marks, and at the completion of the quotation in parentheses you will insert the author, publication year and page number, as follows:

1. Maple (2015) reported, on the basis of his research findings, that "regular gardening activity and health are related" (p. 47), and that the relationship warrants further study.
2. A plea for further research was made by Oak (2013), who reported that "regular gardening activity and health are related" (p. 23), but that the nature of the relationship was unclear.

3. Further study is required by researchers to establish the relationship between "regular gardening activity and health" (Prunus & Magnolia, 2014, p. 54).

Quotations of 40 words or more require a new line. No quotation marks are used and the convention is that the text is indented five spaces on the left hand side. For example, suppose a writer wanted to draw attention to (fictional) findings that had been reported by a researcher. The writer might choose to present the argument through a direct quote as follows:

Cornus (2015, p. 14), reporting on her research into the relationship between regular gardening and elder health, argued:

Researchers in the United Kingdom maintain that regular gardening activity promotes good health in older people. A number of older people have disputed this claim, arguing that their activities in the garden have led to ailments including arthritis and backache. Mary Jones, for example, in her letter to the editor of the *Gardening Times* (1 April 2014), argued that her long-standing interest in maintaining the flower beds around her home has resulted in persistent muscular pain (p. 6). When compared with the health of her non-gardening friends, Ms Jones pointed out that she is far less healthy than they are.

The use of et al.

The abbreviation 'et al.' means 'and others'. For citations with three, four or five authors, you will need to write down each author the first time you cite the reference in-text. When you cite this same reference later, you may simply write the name of the first author followed by 'et al.'. References with six or more authors may be recorded in-text with the use of 'et al.', even for the first time they are noted. One further point to note is that you should never use et al. in the reference list.

Reference lists

It is easiest if some of the conventions are illustrated through a few fictitious examples:

Rose, A. (2013). Eradicating weeds in the garden: The case of unwelcome intruders in the potager. *The Vegetable Garden Enthusiast, 2*(3), 12–23.
Oak, B. F., & Maple, T. E. (2012). *Eco-friendly gardening in city landscapes* (2nd ed.). New York, NY: Alternative Publications.
Tulip, H. (2010). *The effects on the body of constant gardening activity* (Unpublished doctoral dissertation). University of Gardenland.

Plotting, D. E. (2009). *A novice's guide to garden design.* Paper presented at the NGGD 2014 Conference held in conjunction with the 3rd Designers' Discussion Group, Sydney, Australia.

Landscape Development Department. (2010). *The weekend gardener's guide: Blooming beautiful.* Manchester, England: Ministry of Landscape Development.

Sheers, H. (2012). Hedges, trees and vines. *Journal of Autumn Pruning, 13*(2), 56-68.

Climber, H. (2012). The relationship between knowledge of plant botanical names and social status. In A. B. High & M. A. Class (Eds.), *Making it amongst your peers* (pp. 142-156). Charlotte, NC: American Social Standing Convention.

Petunia, N. (2007). *Review of research on colour in the flower beds.* http://www.aaa.bbb/ npetunia/net/colourflowerbeds-summary.html

Pansy, T. R., & Poppy, K. C. (2011). Linking horticultural activity with the delay of heart disease onset. In L. Daffodil (Ed.), *Proceedings of the 23rd Conference of the Horticulture Research Group of Spain* (Vol. 3, pp. 9-21). Barcelona, Spain: Spanish Inquisition of Horticulture.

Toronto Ministry of Horticultural Development. (2012). *Hobbyists' guidelines.* Toronto: Author.

Elm, T. (2014, January 12). Regular gardening promotes good health. *The Standard* (Perth, Australia), p. 10.

Revising your literature review

Revising and editing are key tasks and you need to allow plenty of time for this process. Read through the literature review with critical eyes. Read what is actually on the page not what you thought you had written. Start with the big picture of the literature review and your key argument and check out the structure, looking for consistency across sections. In the finer details, ask yourself if you have over- or under-explained an important point. Try not to be too precious about your literature review but be prepared to prune, elaborate or reorganize so that the reader will be able to share your meaning. When the writing has been revised then you can begin to edit.

During editing you will need to pay attention to grammar and spelling, and look for typographical errors. Many postgraduate researchers have learned not to rely on the spelling and grammar checks provided by the software on their computers. Be sure that your punctuation is correct, that you use apostrophes appropriately, and that your verb tenses are appropriate. Check your references. Most of all, check for evidence of and correct your habitual errors. Sloppy presentation is easy to avoid. It is critically important that you do so because it will tend to cloud the reader's thinking, giving the impression that the literature review has been undertaken carelessly. Seek the advice of your advisors or supervisors and use their experience to assess whether your literature review engages critically with the debates around your topic and allows you to be considered as a credible researcher.

INSIGHTS FROM A REVIEWER

"The literature review identifies four sources of challenge to the integration of citizenry agendas in the formation of environmental policy by local governments. In its comprehensive review of the local literature, the author persuasively argues that scholarship to date has focused on institutional structures and substantive issues, tending to leave actors' perspectives relatively unexplored. These perspectives are defined as 'underlying subjective values, perceptions and preferences that bear on the formation of actors' agendas'. The review thus convincingly identifies the contribution the research seeks to make. The focus on what might be called the more cultural dimension of politics makes a welcome addition to current local scholarship."

Review

Main points

- The literature review is a significant component of all research.
- It is through your writing that you communicate your research to others.
- Support groups can assist by offering constructive feedback on your writing.
- The literature review demonstrates your command of what has been written on and around your topic.
- Your review demonstrates that you are capable of adding a contribution to this body of work.
- Headings and sub-headings in the literature review introduce new themes and serve to break up the extensive content for ease of reading.
- Your central argument is threaded through your literature review.
- The reader is guided through the reading.
- Each paragraph has only one key message.
- Clear transitional sentences or words enhance a reader's engagement with your work.
- The literature review is ongoing throughout the research.
- The importance of revision and editing is not to be underestimated.

Key Terms

- Literature review
- Argument
- Communication

Looking ahead

The next chapter looks at research designs and discusses how different kinds of research demand different kinds of methodological tools. The chapter explores a range of data collection methods and a range of data analysis methods typically employed in social science research. It considers the selection of a research site and the recruitment of participants for the research, and pays attention to the recording and transcribing of data collected.

5 Defining a Research Methodology

Research designs

By now you will have discovered that research is quite an orderly and systematic process. Decisions over the topic, the research questions, and the literature all follow quite logically one to the other. You first need to identify your topic. You then clarify your research questions by reading the literature, and when these are firmed up and you have developed your conceptual framework, you are in a strong position to write your literature review. Things tend to proceed more or less logically. The same is true of the decisions you make about how you will gather and analyze your data. There is logic to those decisions.

Looking back, in developing your research questions and in couching your work within a specific conceptual framework, you prepared the ground for thinking about the kind of research design required. Let's think about the research design in the same way as we view the design of a house. It's a plan. It's systematic and logical and it's guaranteed to make the building stand firm. The owner might have commissioned a design for any number of purposes. For example, it might be a building plan for a holiday house, or a large family home, or an apartment. It might be a plan for a factory. It depends on the owner's purpose for the building. In the same way, your research design will fit the purpose of your research. Different purposes initiate different research designs, and if the fit is good, your research design will hold your research together.

Not only do different purposes initiate different designs, different research requirements also lead to design variation. In our building plan, many possible designs for buildings of the same purpose are possible. Before the plan can be drawn up for a family home, for example, the owners will have addressed fundamental questions concerning the family's needs. They will have considered their specific requirements in terms of the number of levels, the number of bedrooms, the approximate size of the living space and so on. Then there are the finer details, such as the location of the refrigerator in the kitchen, and the owners will need to make decisions on these as well.

In the same way, individual research designs for the same purpose will vary in the detail. Before the design can take shape, questions ranging from the broad to the specific will need to be addressed. Consider the question: Are you fascinated more by numbers, historical documents, ideas, people or initiating change? Your answer will influence your design. Now let's turn to the research questions. What data will need to be collected, from whom and where and when? How will the data be collected and analyzed? When you make these decisions with careful thought, your design will provide a coherent plan for undertaking your research. It will demonstrate a conceptual integrity between the purpose of your research and your decisions concerning the information and data needed, the ways in which you will collect and analyze the data, the numbers of kinds of participants in your study, and how you will report the findings.

The decisions that you make in your design are not to be taken lightly. They will influence the kinds and level of findings you obtain and, hence, will significantly influence the conclusions that you are able to draw. If constructed carefully and rigorously, both at this stage and iteratively through the data collection and analysis process, the research design will not only offer a logical plan for your study, it will also supply you with appropriate and adequate evidence to answer your research questions effectively and efficiently. It will guarantee that your research will stand up to scrutiny.

Research design purposes

Different designs develop from different research purposes. Each provides a structure so that specific kinds of questions can be addressed. Every research purpose asks a different kind of research question.

- What is going on?
- What is the solution?
- How can this be explained more clearly?
- How can this be improved?
- How effective is this?

Each kind of question provides direction for your design. This is an opportune time for you to address the purpose of your research.

Identifying the specific purpose of your intended research allows an appropriate research design to become clearer. For example, if you have an inclination towards numbers then you may well be interested in a survey design. If historical documents fascinate you then a genealogical design

Case Study 5.1

FATIMA'S RESEARCH

Digital technology use within a quilting circle

Fatima was interested in the use of digital technology amongst mature women. The particular context for her research was a quilting circle that met regularly every month. Although she had formulated her research question and had delved into the literature with it in mind, she wanted to reassure herself that her question was exactly what she wanted to answer. In brainstorming all the ways she could think of to explore this topic, she came up with the following:

WAYS OF EXPLORING DIGITAL TECHNOLOGY USE IN A QUILTING CIRCLE				
Understanding	Solving	Changing	Evaluating	Theorizing
What is going on?	What is the solution?	How can this be improved?	How effective is this?	How can this be explained more clearly?
Do women make use of technology during the quilting activity and if so, how, why and when?	How could technology be used productively within the quilting circle?	How could women be encouraged to use technology more to assist in their quilting activities?	How has the introduction of technology within the quilting circle changed productivity?	How can we offer a new explanation of the use of technology in women's quilting activities?

Fatima was not interested in changing the quilting environment in relation to technology use. In addition, she thought that her technological expertise did not extend to finding out ways in which technology could be used within the circle. She knew that she would find it difficult to come up with new explanations for the women's use of technology at the group's regular meetings. What she really wanted to find out was when and for what purpose the women used technology. She considered a case study of the quilting circle would be appropriate for her interest.

may frame your study (Howell and Prevenier, 2001). If you consider yourself a deep thinker, then a theoretical design may appeal. If people are of primary interest, then a case study design (Yin, 2011) or an ethnographic design may be of interest. If you consider yourself a change agent then a design incorporating action research (Somekh, 2006) may well be appropriate. The applicability of each design will now be explained further.

If you are keenly interested in understanding something or some people, and in fathoming out what is going on, your design orientation will probably be *case study* and/or *ethnographic*. For example, a researcher might be interested in finding out how students experience empathy in an on-line nursing course. The researcher might explore the experiences of the students and perhaps the lecturer within one class, which would then become the 'case' to be studied. A truly ethnographic study of this case would require the researcher's direct observations (Adler and Adler, 1994) of what the on-line experience of empathy might be for the students and the teacher over a sustained period of time.

If your interest is in solving a puzzle and finding a solution, then you might be also be drawn to a *case study design*. For example, suppose you were interested in community sport and recreation, with particular focus on developing facilities that meet the present and future needs of the local community. Your local community would become your 'case', and your research might centre on understanding community members' sport and recreation needs and their views of the current and proposed facilities.

Thinking carefully through your research purpose, objective or aim, will help clarify your research orientation. If theorizing and explaining things in a new way is your objective, then you will have a more *theoretical* or *philosophical* orientation. If you want to change and improve a situation, your orientation is likely to be *action research*. Suppose your interest was centred on improving workplace systems to make them more responsive to technological innovations, then you might research the evolution of workplace practices under the influence of a change agent.

If exploring differences in events over time is of primary interest, then you might be drawn to an *historical* (Howell and Prevenier, 2001) or *longitudinal* design (Menard, 1991). For example, you might want to explore the effectiveness of different local body voting systems in your area over a 20-year period. Financial costs and voters' experiences might be two factors that you explore. If the evaluation of a new initiative is your objective then you might be drawn to an *experimental* design (Patton, 2002). As an example, you might want to evaluate the effectiveness of a different adult reading programme offered to new settlers in your community. You might assess the difference in effectiveness between a current reading programme with one group of adult readers and a newly introduced reading initiative with another group.

In the above examples, each of the research purposes generated a different research design, and each design provided a possible structure for addressing specific kinds of questions.

Activity

EXPLORING MY PROPOSED RESEARCH

1. What is the key purpose or main objective of your research?
2. What *kinds* of questions does it ask?
3. What type of study do your research questions logically demand?

Research methodology

Designs do not simply appear out of thin air. They are built on theoretical foundations. Your methodology represents an overarching framework for your orientation and your procedures. It signals the philosophy underpinning what you plan to do in your research. In Chapter 2 we discussed how every piece of academic research is based on a worldview. Different worldviews are linked to different assumptions. In academic research, when you plan and undertake research you buy into a set of assumptions that fits a particular worldview. Research never happens in a vacuum. Your methodology signals your assumptions about the form and nature of the reality being studied. It also signals your assumptions about appropriate ways of developing knowledge of that reality.

These different standpoints shape the way reality is viewed and the way in which the notion of truth is understood. Each provides a framework and a grounding for the way in which the study will be conducted, as in the examples given above:

Study	Framework	Design
Adult reading programme	Positivist	Experimental
Empathy	Interpretivist	Ethnographic
Workplace	Emancipatory	Action research

We can think of each of these frameworks as giving direction to as well as grounding the study. This is the known as the methodology. It influences the nature of the research design and, as part of that, the gathering and the analysis of data.

Designs founded on positivism are generally known as quantitative research designs. They involve both intervention and non-intervention research and include experimental research, correlational research and survey research (Shadish, Cook and Campbell, 2002). The design follows a linear, sequential and deductive process for proving or disproving hypotheses. Quantitative designs are in the business of testing theories. They look at facts, numbers and measurement and focus on convergences, as well as variation within a specific dimension or variable across and within a given population and situation. Quantitative methods enable the 'impartial' and 'detached' researcher to investigate a wide range of areas but typically at the surface level rather than in-depth. Experiments and closed questionnaires are examples of instruments that might be used in such designs.

Supposing we were interested in female CEOs in very large companies in the United States: how many there were, their ages, where they were located, what their work entailed. A quantitative design would allow us to find out those details. We might decide to use an on-line questionnaire and post it to every company over a certain size in the US. We would need to be sure that the scope of the survey questions was sufficiently broad to allow us to gather all the information of interest to us, since all the data would be collected in this one instance. We would be looking at the data for patterns that could be generalized, and from which we might make predictions for the future. Our analysis would offer a broad, but focused, overview of female CEOs in very large US companies. We would be able to report similarities in the demographics, and convergence of their work experiences. In statistical terms we would be reporting measures of 'central tendency'. We would also want to report on variations within the data. These data are known as 'measures of dispersion'.

Designs based on interpretivism are known as qualitative research designs. They include explorations of cultures, groups of people and individuals. The purpose is to look in-depth at what is going on holistically, in an evolving and circular way. The focus, then, is on 'texture' – in exploring how separate parts and their interconnections contribute to a cohesive entity. A wide range of studies draw on interpretivist designs, from the highly theoretical to the deeply empirical, such as a sociolinguistics study of conversations. Whatever the format, these designs are inductive and do not rely on numbers or measurements. Interviews (King and Horrocks, 2010) and focus groups (Morgan, 1997) are sometimes used as data collection methods in these designs. Interpretivist designs may also be founded on emancipatory principles.

As an example of a qualitative design, consider again our study on female CEOs in very large companies. Suppose we were interested in the past work experiences of the women and in how those experiences contributed to their current positions. We would be looking closely and intently at influences in the development of female CEOs. We might opt for individual interviews with a small group of such women, with the understanding that the researcher's involvement in the interviews is not impartial. As information during the interview is shared by individual participants, the researcher may explore new lines of inquiry. It is likely that each of the women's narratives will be unique, hence generalization of experiences to the wider group of female CEOs may be difficult. However, the report we produce will celebrate diversity and difference, offering rich insights from the working lives of individual women.

Mixed method research designs (Cresswell, 2009) combine both qualitative and quantitative research procedures. Data from the separate designs are integrated or mixed. When used in social science research to study human phenomena, they are offered at both the level of overall inquiry design and the level of data collection methods. Their use might involve a mixed approach, such as a survey design combined with a case study or an action research design. With regard to methods, the mixed design might involve the use of quantitative procedures to gather and analyze numeric data and the use of qualitative procedures to collect and explain descriptions of human behaviour. Typically, when the mixed methods design is used to represent human phenomena in social science research, open-ended interviews and/or unstructured observations are offered to provide a complementary voice to questionnaires (Maxwell and Loomis, 2003; Mertens, 2005; Morse, 2003).

For example, our study of female CEOs of very large companies might incorporate a mixed methods design which pairs a national survey with individual interviews from a representative sample of women. The survey provides baseline quantitative data from multiple and varied perspectives and the interviews offer perspectives at a deeper level. The researcher then merges the two sources of data together. The researcher may have particular purposes in mind. She might justify the use of the design on the grounds of any of the following:

- greater generalizability of findings,
- stronger validity or credibility,
- more reliable triangulation of data deeper and more comprehensive understanding of human phenomena.

A look at a range of designs

Ethnography

Ethnographic designs represent procedures for writing about people. The term 'ethnography' is applied to a range of studies, typically requiring the researcher's direct involvement with a group in its natural setting (Guba and Lincoln, 1985). Ethnographic studies are founded on the notion of people as meaning makers (Bochner and Ellis, 2002). Such studies emphasize that what people say and do are both informed by the meanings they construct, in collaboration with others, of their cultural world. The focus, then, is on understanding the complex and dynamic cultural world. In particular, the interest relates to the personal and social, that is, on how people interpret and use their everyday world's realities (Hughes, Pennington and Makris, 2012).

Ethnographic studies engage with the qualitative design purposes of developing theories. They are not concerned with testing established hypotheses. Honouring the participants' agency in meaning making, such studies use a variety of data-gathering procedures, such as prolonged observation of the setting, document and artefact analysis, and interviewing members of the culture. They draw on the group's historical context as a backdrop to finding out and documenting in-the-moment as much as possible about its

Case Study 5.2

SAM'S ETHNOGRAPHIC RESEARCH

Sam was interested in understanding the life, culture and behaviour of a small group of young adults in a privately-funded residential programme for drug and alcohol rehabilitation. He planned to research one group for the duration of the programme, observing, listening to what was said, and gathering any other relevant data that was made available to him. He took steps to ensure that his presence and his methods were sensitive to the context and to the participants within that context.

everyday life. But the design is not likely to be fixed at the planning stage because new interests may emerge that initiate new lines of inquiry or sharpen their focus as the research proceeds. The researcher's decision-making regarding data collection is necessarily in a state of flux, but it will be informed by the kind of data they hoped to collect.

Case studies

A case study has no single universal design structure (Yin, 2003). Like ethnographic designs, case studies use a range of methods and data sources for understanding human phenomena. Case studies focus attention on a 'case' – one individual, one group, one setting, an activity, or an issue – to learn more about the phenomena under investigation. As with ethnographic designs, a case study design involving participants provides them with a voice and power as experts in the setting. Factual information is typically enhanced with the views of participants for a deeper interrogation of the phenomena being studied.

Unlike ethnographic designs, the case study design may be informed by either quantitative or qualitative design purposes. A case study design might employ only quantitative procedures such as 'objective' observation, or analyses of survey, archival, or systems data to test a theory about the case. More likely, however, in social science research, and depending on the resources available and the boundaries established for the research, the design might use a range of qualitative procedures to emphasize the social construction of meaning. It may also involve mixed methods to identify, describe and analyze in detail the complexity of the case, before determining the fit or otherwise with an existing theory and the literature. Whatever procedures are used, the point is to understand the case more deeply rather than to make general claims that could be applied beyond the case.

Case Study 5.3

EMMA'S CASE STUDY RESEARCH

Emma was interested in exploring a senior management team's approaches to instructional leadership at a school. She planned to determine by interview how the individual members of the team perceived their role as instructional leaders and how their aspirations met the reality of their practice. Her intention was to gather relevant policies and other documentary evidence produced by the school. She also planned to observe a number of senior leadership team meetings.

However, while the findings may not be generalizable, they may be suggestive of what is happening within the population at large.

Action research

Action research (Carr and Kemmis, 1986; Somekh, 2006) designs are action plans for emancipatory purposes. The designs map out systematic procedures to solve real problems and to effect change and improvement. Action research is collaborative research undertaken with people rather than on people. While it can take a number of forms, it will begin with a problem or an issue within a setting and will involve the people within the setting working through a process to bring about change and a new vision. The highly structured process is developed from the understanding that ready-made solutions are inadequate to deal with the complexity of human behaviour and to initiate long-term change. More often than not, the researcher works in collaboration with the group to facilitate change.

As with case study designs, action research designs may be informed by either qualitative or mixed methods design purposes. Although the researcher and the participants may have a clear plan of the current and proposed situation, the approaches taken to shift from one to the other are not fully within the researcher's control. The design will be adapted through a series of spirals that slowly advance action and behaviour in the setting towards the intended goal. In a sense, the design is a plan for trial and error: planning, action, observation, evaluation, re-planning, action, and so forth. More specifically, the cycles begin with a clear identification of the problem, and a shared understanding of 'where we are at and what needs to be done', taking into account the available resources and the time frame. Data collection and analysis and evaluation of the situation will then lead to the development of new theorizing to inform further action and further cycles.

Case Study 5.4

CHLOE'S ACTION RESEARCH

Chloe worked as the manager of a not-for-profit second-hand clothing shop. She was aware that there was a level of tension amongst the volunteers at the shop and wanted to explore how interactions within this small community could become more collegial. An action research project was designed and included a number of cycles of planning, reflecting and evaluation.

Experimental and non-experimental designs

Experimental designs are quantitative procedures used to investigate the effect of an intervention (Shadish et al., 2002). It is an exploration of what happens when one variable is systematically manipulated over another. The manipulated variable – the independent variable – is known as the experimental treatment, and the observed variable is known as the dependent variable. If, as a result of the intervention, outcomes change by more than could be attributed to chance, then we say that a causal relationship exists between the two variables.

Non-experimental designs investigate relationships among variables, rather than manipulate them. Designs that use statistical analysis to determine the relation or association between variables are known as correlational designs. The most commonly used non-experimental designs are survey designs. Survey designs include questionnaires, structured interviews, documents and structured observations, and each is used to collect data from people at a given point in time. Although survey designs are situated among the family of quantitative designs, they tend to be more exploratory in nature. Their purpose is to provide a broad picture or a statement of trends to do with characteristics, features, attitudes, opinions and behaviours of people.

Case Study 5.5

HANNAH'S EXPERIMENTAL DESIGN RESEARCH

Hannah was interested in the effects of teaching the 'times tables' by a new method. She planned for one class in a school to be taught by traditional methods and another, equally matched class in the school to be taught by the new method. Both classes would sit the same pre-test and the same post-test preceding and following the units of work on times tables, and Hannah would compare the results. If there was evidence that the new method produced higher results she could conclude, within certain limitations, that the new method was more effective.

Narrative research designs

Narrative inquiry is focused on personal experiences (Ellis and Bochner, 2000). Informed by qualitative purposes, narrative research designs provide the researcher with the material relating to the experiences and lifestyles of individuals or groups over a period of time through the stories narrated to them. Such designs are particularly influential in research into social change since the data sources offer unique perspectives of the social event under investigation. Because the theoretical perspectives or frames of reference of the participants may well be different from the researcher's, there is a pressing need to make explicit the position of the researcher within the research activity. In some narrative inquiry designs the focus of the research is squarely on the researcher and his or her own personal experiences.

In narrative research designs personal experiences are recorded systematically using both traditional and contemporary methods through the use of artefacts, video diaries, interviews, journals, letters and so forth. A number of issues demand attention, and these relate to the issue of storying oneself through time and the problem of accounting for historical events. In addition, the economic and cultural context for the story must be made explicit. Then there's the issue of reflection. What does the story teller choose to say and what does he or she choose not to say? There is also, for the researcher, the issue of emotions and how the story teller articulates feelings and dreams to confront.

Case Study 5.6

NOAH'S NARRATIVE RESEARCH

Noah wanted to explore the life story of an eminent heart surgeon. He considered that there might be significant events and influences in the story that could offer important guidance for medical students and others. Noah planned to conduct multiple interviews with the surgeon in order to understand his life and to contextualize the personal story with relevant documentary data.

Historical research designs

Historical research, undertaken carefully, is both descriptive and analytical (Howell and Prevenier, 2001). It not only describes events and behaviours, it also offers a critical interrogation. The purpose is to learn from history in order to fill a gap in our knowledge, and, often, to understand the present. Historical research does more than offer facts and figures; it offers a story about the past that involves social, cultural and, possibly, emotional experiences. As with narrative inquiry designs, historical research is highly interpretive and hence is informed by qualitative underpinnings in relation to the construction of social, cultural and political meanings. Interpretation operates at a number of levels, including the material the researcher chooses to select or reject as data and the ways in which the data are constructed in the write-up.

The historical researcher typically works with primary and secondary sources of material and aims for accuracy, authenticity and completeness. Primary sources offer first-hand public or private evidence of the phenomena being studied. Multiple primary sources might be drawn upon by the researcher, and these include interviews with key informants, letters, official documents, archival material, emails and journals, even down to the sketchy notes of those directly implicated in the event under investigation. Secondary sources add depth to the study by offering previously analyzed primary material from biographies, newspaper reports, commentaries, and so on. All these sources need to be interpreted and constructed in a critical way to provide a fuller picture and better insights into the historical event.

Case Study 5.7

LOUIS' HISTORICAL RESEARCH

Louis was interested in exploring how the concept of standards for reading, writing and mathematics changed over time. He was particularly interested in why those changes happened and who influenced those changes. He planned to delve into archival documents, records of parliamentary debates, and media reports for his data.

Grounded theory designs

Grounded theory designs are further examples of designs based on interpretivism. They are systematic qualitative procedures for exploring people and processes (Charmaz, 2003). The objective is to draw on the perceptions of people in order to generate a theory that might explain what is going on in a holistic way. More precisely, the researcher analyzes the data inductively and this leads to new associations amongst concepts and new questions which, in turn, lead to additional data collection. The iterative process results in the generation of theory. Grounded theory, then, is a theory grounded in the perceptions of people. Although they have their own design purposes, both ethnographic and narrative research are sometimes considered as examples of grounded theory designs.

As with the researcher involved in action research, the grounded theory researcher may have a plan for the research, yet the design is more likely to emerge as a result of careful reflection and evaluation of the initial data collection and analysis. Typically, the design procedures involve observing and interviewing, and then categorizing data according to themes. Once the data are interpreted, they may be represented in the form of diagrams or models as a means of explaining the theory.

Case Study 5.8

HILARY'S GROUNDED THEORY RESEARCH

Hilary wanted to investigate nursing students' knowledge of decision-making and clinical problem-solving at the beginning of their nursing tertiary education. She wanted to use grounded theory to generate a new substantive theory around their prior experiences. Her plan was to interview students and their teachers.

We have looked at a number of possible designs for research. Since there is a wide range of design options available to you, you will need to be sure that the overall design you choose will allow you to address your research questions.

Activity

MY RESEARCH DESIGN

Consider again the research you are expecting to undertake.

1. What overall research design would enable you to meet the key purpose of your research?
2. How will your chosen design help you meet the key purpose of your research?
3. Why have you not chosen any of the other designs described above?

Data collection methods

The research design you have chosen will steer you towards the kinds of datasets that would enable you to address your research questions. You will need to be sure that your chosen methodological track will generate appropriate and reliable data of sufficient quantity and suitable quality for your analysis. There are no hard-and-fast rules about the kinds of data you should gather for any given design. However, different research designs tend to indicate specific kinds of datasets. Suppose your topic area was nursing practices in the battlefield during the First World War, then your historical research design would suggest you need to access patient records, archival documents, historical camera footage and so on.

Research methods are the approaches that you will take to gather and analyze your data (Cohen, Manion and Morrison, 2007). The data collection methods most helpful in your research are those which open up access to the phenomenon you are studying. You are trying to make sound methodological decisions that will create a strong logical flow within your plan. Your methodological framework will point to the use of some data collection and analysis methods, and not others.

By now it should be clear which data types would not be appropriate. In the wartime nursing example, it is unlikely that you would want to carry out observations or use videoing to gather your data. Similarly, if you were evaluating a new nursing instructional method it is likely that you would be more interested in data relating to nursing students' test results and perhaps students' perceptions following the application of the method than you would be in gathering archival data. The data collection methods you choose will depend on what you want to find out and who you want to find it out from. The ones that will be most useful to you are those which provide direct access to the phenomenon you are studying. Sound methodological decisions create a strong logical flow within your research design. They enable strong connections between the methodological framework and the techniques applied to data collection and analysis, ensuring that the design is reliable, rigorous and valid for addressing your research questions.

You will also need to confront the issue of scale and the resources you have available for the project – both material and time. Addressing these questions systematically will help you avoid under-collection or over-collection of data. Without careful thought and deliberate planning, it will be too easy to overlook an important data source. It will be too late at the analysis and writing stages of your workplace study, for example, when you realize you should have interviewed the team manager as well as the team, or when you become aware that you neglected to ask the team an important question. Similarly, it will be easy to become distracted in the field so that you end up collecting superfluous data that stray into other 'interesting' research areas. Much as you might justify collecting this set of data on the basis that it might come in useful, remember to keep your research questions squarely within focus. A focus on the research questions will help you make the really hard decisions concerning the most useful and critical data that will provide convincing and reliable evidence.

While you are attending to the issues concerning too few and too many data sources, you need to give due consideration to the answers you expect from your research question. Then ask yourself how you plan to analyze the answers you expect to collect. This point is important because the decisions you make concerning your data analysis tools will influence the kind of data you need to collect. A common mistake amongst postgraduate researchers is in trying to figure out what to do with the data *after* it has been collected. Ask yourself early on: what kind of data will yield the response I expect to get from my research questions and how do I propose to analyze that dataset?

There are a number of big decisions relating to your data collection that you will need to resolve. Suppose, for example, your design is experimental and you are interested in the effects of a new teaching strategy in the classroom. However, you want to be sure that student aptitude is controlled in the experiment so as not to distort the effects of the teaching strategy. You might decide to use a standardized, established instrument such as a scholastic aptitude test to provide you with students' scores. Reliance on standardized *instruments* is common practice in quantitative designs.

Other designs rely more on self-developed *protocols.* For example, in investigating the types of recreation facilities required in a local retirement village, you might expect, given the mobility restrictions of these people, more sedentary activities to feature high on the requirement list. Of course, you would want to ask the elderly people themselves for their views on their sport and recreation needs. A needs assessment might be undertaken through a survey to gauge the community's requirements. The assessment might also be undertaken through individual or focus group interviews. Or, you might use both survey and interviews. Do you have the resources and skills to develop and analyze a survey and interview data? Will the analyses provide you with answers to your research questions?

In addition to survey and interview, the methods of data collection that are available in social science research activity include observation and non-obtrusive methods, to gather the data sources from government, agency and archival records collection, the internet, newspapers, magazines, artefacts and so forth. Data tools are those that assist with the data collection. These include questionnaires, focus groups, tests, observation checklists and records, interview schedules, written, audio and video recordings, and journals. You might want to combine the tools and use a questionnaire for a broad understanding of your topic area, and interviews to find out more in-depth information about your area of interest. Adding observations at the research site to the mix will provide you with the means of triangulating and verifying the data.

Looking briefly at the first of these three data collection methods, surveys aim to capture attitudes, values, behaviour, preferences and the like at a particular point in time. You will be familiar with surveys consisting of a series of questions, usually relating to a specific issue, administered on-line, through postal mail or telephone, or in person. There are a number of considerations for the researcher to address. First, if a questionnaire is used, practical considerations such as user-friendliness in terms of presentation, instructions, language, tone, layout, space for responses, are all highly important. Second, the questions, and the order they appear in the questionnaire, need to be thought through very carefully. Be warned that the questions will take you longer to construct than you anticipate. Third, if you are surveying a small group from a wider population, your sample will need to be generated through appropriate sampling techniques in order for you to generalize your findings to the wider population.

Interviews, on the other hand, are a means to gaining an in-depth understanding of the human phenomena being studied. They may be conducted with individuals or with focus groups. They may consist of structured, unstructured or semi-structured formats. Unstructured interviews offer flexible approaches to interviewing (Seidman, 2006) by allowing the participant to shape the content of the discussion. It is a particularly useful approach when exploring a complex domain or when the domain is not well known. In individual interviewing settings, photo elicitation is sometimes used, particularly within anthropology and sociology, to focus the discussion. The photos, taken by either the individual or the interviewer, serve as a prompt for a discussion and offer the interviewee an opportunity to provide his or her interpretation of what the photos mean. When the interviewee rather than the interviewer has taken the photos, an opportunity is provided for the individual to explain, qualify and justify their choice of images.

Structured and semi-structured interview formats guide the participants' discussion more closely. In focus group interviews the researcher acts as facilitator, aiming to elicit a wide range of views, to provide participants with greater thinking and reflection time than might be possible through individual interviewing, and to gain insight from the group's interaction. The researcher needs to be alert to power and cultural issues within the group and must ensure that the group's interaction remains evenly balanced. In both individual and focus group interviews, the interviews may be audio or video recorded or may be recorded through notes or checklists. A recording check is essential, as is a brief pre-interview familiarization meeting to establish rapport, trust and confidence with participants.

Observations offer another data collection technique. They consist of either structured or unstructured formats. In quantitative research designs, the observation is recorded on highly structured schedules that categorize behaviours into small segments over equal time units. In qualitative research designs (Denzin and Lincoln, 2008), observations are unstructured in the sense that the observer is listening and looking for more general behaviours that represent responses to bigger questions. The observations are typically recorded through field notes or video files. They provide a valuable resource as they enable reconstruction of participant experience in context. The researcher first needs to develop a high level of trust with the participants. Second, the researcher needs to work within the regularities and routines of the research site and act unobtrusively – like a 'fly on the wall'. While in some research situations the participants quickly overlook the fact that the researcher or camera is observing, in other situations, the participants may behave in an atypical manner because of the presence of the researcher or camera.

Irrespective of the data collection method(s) you plan to use, you will be employing those method(s) to source data that will provide an entrée into new understandings. By now you will have figured out the kind of data that will yield the response you expect to get from your research questions. But what about the data that does not provide the kind of response you expect? This dataset is too important to ignore. Simply because it challenges your ideal dataset does not give you cause to ignore it. It will provide a powerful counter-story and allow you to offer more complete and richer findings than would otherwise be possible.

Data analysis

Now you have a clear sense of how you will gather your data. Once the data have been collected they will need to be processed. The methods that you use to gather and analyze the data are, taken together, known as the research methods. While data gathering is fundamental to an empirical study, the importance of the analysis is not to be understated. It forms the key link between your data and your conclusions. Systematic analytical methods lead to sound results and findings, which then form the basis of the conclusions you draw. Rigorous and appropriate data analytical methods are the goal because they will generate confidence in your findings.

There are many ways of looking at a set of data. One researcher might be intrigued by some aspects of the data, while another will bring another perspective of social reality to the same dataset. The sheer complexity of human phenomena allows you to put your unique interpretation on the richness of social life. There is no one right way to interpret data but, having said that, there are some methods that will follow on logically from your research questions and data collection methods. Some analytical methods will have a greater fit within your research design than others. If, for example, your research involves an historical design, then your analysis might call for a content analysis which examines the content of official documents, diaries, letters, essays, personal notes, media reports and so forth. Alternatively, your design might suggest a Foucauldian analysis (Walshaw, 2007) that looks more deeply at written texts to explore the relationship between knowledge and forms of power and agency. If your design was ethnographic then you might be interested in discourse analysis to explore how participants use, interpret and reproduce language (Potter and Wetherell, 1987) to convey specific experiences and meanings.

You will need to sort the data into patterns or themes that relate in some way to your research questions. Unless your coding framework was pre-specified, you may want to consider using a visual approach, such as a concept map, to assist you. Alternatively, you might use a software package to help with the organization of your data into themes or key factors. Of course, any computer program will require direction from you. Thematic clustering, whether assisted electronically or otherwise, is necessarily inferential and interpretive. Numerical data also need to be assembled and collated. A number of software packages are available to assist in the statistical analysis of your data and they will provide displays of the data in compact form such as tables, charts, diagrams and graphs. However, these data displays and analyses are not an end in themselves; the findings they generate require your explanation and interpretation in the context of your study.

Be mindful that your analytic methods should allow you to produce a meaningful and plausible discussion that contributes to the wider scholarly debate and relates to what others have already found. Above all, you will want your analytic methods to demonstrate a scholarly rigour that will generate confidence in your findings.

Activity

MY DATA COLLECTION AND DATA ANALYSIS

Consider again the research you are hoping to do.

1. What data collection and analysis methods are appropriate for addressing your research questions?
2. In what ways will your chosen research methods help you address your questions?
3. What are the limitations of your chosen methods?
4. What other research methods would be appropriate for your particular research project?
5. Why did you not choose these other methods?
6. Explain how your research methods fit the central purpose of your research.

Review

Main points

- Different research purposes initiate different research designs.
- A well thought-out design provides a coherent plan for undertaking research.
- All research designs are built on worldviews which frame the way the study will be conducted.
- The overall design will allow you to address your research questions.
- Different research designs tend to lend support to specific kinds of datasets.
- Survey, interview and observations are often used to gather data.
- Some analytical methods will fit better within your design than others.
- Carefully considered analytic methods generate confidence in your findings.

Key Terms

- Research design
- Research methodology
- Research methods

Looking ahead

In the next chapter we shift the focus to the development of the research proposal. The topic, research questions, literature and design of the study are brought together in a structured way to establish a clear articulation of the planned research. The chapter explores the presentation of a research plan as a proposal that is deemed satisfactory for a proposal panel.

6 Creating a Research Proposal

What is a research proposal?

The research proposal is a central feature in the world of academic investigation, and an important step in the research process. The proposal represents a plan for the research, and signals the researcher's intentions by outlining the specific way in which the research will be undertaken. Your proposal will clarify what topic is going to be investigated, what you are trying to achieve, why the research is important, and what processes and procedures you plan to use. But it will do more than demonstrate that you have thought carefully and clearly about what will be investigated and what it will take to successfully complete the investigation. Your successful proposal will demonstrate your potential as a researcher – that you have the necessary knowledge and ability to undertake the research.

The proposal is the formal means by which you step into the apprenticeship of becoming an academic researcher. It is likely that you will be required to formally present, within a given time period, a case for your plans for conducting your research. Invariably, a panel or committee will assess your plans and provide you with helpful feedback. The panel will expect to find sufficient evidence that your proposed research question has merit and that you are capable of pursuing it. They want to be sure that the issue you propose to investigate is sufficiently significant, and that you have allocated an appropriate amount of time and effort to the research.

Essentially, then, in writing the proposal, you are trying to convince a committee (who may not be familiar with your topic) that your research needs to proceed. In developing an argument for your intended research you are, in reality, trying to 'sell' your project by justifying your carefully reasoned and consistent decisions. You are also trying to convince the committee that you are the right person to carry out the research. You need to do that through your engagement with the literature, your methodological argument and your knowledge of the methods. Last, but by no means least, the quality of the writing in your proposal will play a significant role in convincing others of your project's merits. If you are able to persuade the panel, then your proposal will be accepted as a plan for the conduct of research. Once you have obtained any necessary ethical clearances your data collection can start.

One thing that postgraduate researchers quickly learn from developing a research proposal is that, like the literature review, the proposal itself is a form of research. It represents an opportunity to clarify your thinking and firm up on ideas. Explaining and justifying your proposed study to readers and demonstrating its value is an important exercise in your research journey. It will require a clear conceptual framework to put forward a case for your study. It demands thinking, searching, sourcing material and making firm decisions about a range of significant issues that will contribute to your study. The Activities in the earlier chapters gave you an opportunity to make a number of decisions which are critical to your study, and all these decisions will give you a head start in developing the proposal.

You cannot construct a research proposal without first attending to the decisions you made earlier in your journey. That is why this discussion on research proposals is situated after the chapters on literature reviews and methodologies. In the development of your proposal it will be advisable to seek guidance and support from advisors or supervisors. Once firm decisions have been made, the task of producing the proposal becomes very manageable. In fact, many postgraduate researchers look back on this stage as the first time that everything about the project begins to come together.

Requirements of a research proposal

The proposal provides a basic outline of your entire research. Once accepted, the proposal becomes a document to which you can refer in order to inform your work at all stages of the project. But what is involved in developing the proposal? Irrespective of topic area and discipline, your research proposal will read like an essay that offers the basic outline of your intended research. So that readers can make sense of the argument you put forward, it is most important that you write the proposal in plain language. If your writing is too obscure or too 'slap-dash' readers will have difficulty understanding what you plan to do. A well-written proposal clarifies your plans in a way that allows readers to follow the development from research problem to research answer. It will help readers to understand your intentions and how your research will contribute to knowledge.

Some universities require you to submit your proposal on an official template with predetermined headings. Others leave the format to you. However, if the format is of your choosing, you will still be expected to identify what issue your proposed research will investigate, how you will go about addressing the issue, what will be learned, and why you consider it is important to carry out the research. Regulations at some universities require you to defend your proposal orally at a specifically convened meeting. Most universities will require that your proposal is endorsed by your supervisors. Bear in mind, however, that gaining supervisors' approval does not absolve you of full responsibility for the proposal submitted.

Activity

KEY RESEARCH TERMS

Check out the research proposal requirements that must be satisfied for your qualification.

In particular:

1. When will the proposal need to be submitted?
2. Is there a template or standard form to be used?
3. What is the word limit for the proposal?
4. Are specific headings required?
5. Are advisors'/supervisors' signatures required to endorse the proposal?
6. Are you required to defend the proposal?

The point to keep in mind is that you must adhere to the requirements set by your university. Keep as close as possible to the recommended sections or headings. Do not exceed the word limits. If, for example, you are advised that the word limit of the title is 20 words, and that the abstract word limit is 100 words, then be sure not to stretch these limits. If you can follow the proposal guidelines, then it is often assumed that you can probably follow through on what you propose to do in your study. Following guidelines could well be your first big test in the research stakes. Be sure, first, that you know what is expected of you, and second, that you do not deviate from the requirements.

Sections often included in a research proposal

Your proposal will need a clear organizational structure so that a panel of non-experts in your field can understand what is planned. That means it should be written in a user-friendly way. It will need a table of contents that lists the sections in the order they appear in the proposal and the page number on which each section can be found. Do not overlook the importance of the table of contents for clarifying the focus and approach of the proposed study. Within the body of the proposal, the various sections need to fit together well. They should be organized in such a way that you are able to clarify the aim of the research, justify the research, set it within the context of relevant literature, outline your data collection and analysis methods, explain who will participate, describe the resources needed and the time-frame, and outline the contribution to knowledge that the project will make.

However the proposal needs to do more than describe, it needs to clarify the logic behind your decisions. You can provide that clarity in each of the sections when you know precisely what the purpose of each section is. It might be to set the scene or to describe what you actually plan to do and with whom, or it might be to document the resources needed and so on. Developing the proposal in a way that responds to the purpose will provide better communication between you and the reader. By shifting your focus onto the purpose and what the reader is looking for, your proposal will become more convincing.

Let's look in some detail at the purposes of individual headings.

CHECKLIST OF POSSIBLE SECTIONS FOR RESEARCH PROPOSALS

1. Title
2. Abstract
3. Introduction
4. Aims and objectives
5. Research questions
6. Conceptual framework and theory
7. Literature review
8. Methodology
9. Significance
10. Limitations
11. Ethical issues
12. Timetable
13. References
14. Appendices (e.g., protocols, budget, resources)

These are the headings that are often used in research proposals. However, researchers do not always work on the proposal sections in the order shown. The introduction is a case in point. It provides a summary of background information, definitions, context, summary of past research, and a rationale for the study. Some researchers choose to clarify their thinking by working on subsequent sections and then writing the introducion. While working on one section it is likely that others will change or be refined so that various 'parts' of the proposal are 'overlapping' in your mind. Your final proposal will have sound integrity with all the various sections fitting together well. In actual fact, you have probably achieved that 'whole' by developing it piece-meal.

Proposals need a clear statement of purpose and a well-planned literature review which typically begins with the broad topic and gradually narrows the focus. Moreover, proposals need a research question(s) and possibly sub-questions, a research design, a proposed analytical framework, and a discussion on limitations and ethics in relation to the conduct of the study. We will consider the components of the research proposal and their function in more detail.

Title

The title gives the reader a clear sense of what you are investigating. The words you choose in your title should provide as much information in as few words as possible about the content and context of your research. That is to say, your title should be carefully chosen to include some key words that encapsulate succinctly, unambiguously, and in a compelling manner, the nature of your research.

Abstract

An abstract is provided as a summary of the key features of the research. It is often restricted to around 100 words that identify the topic, purpose, theory, methodology and significance of the study, as well as the argument underwriting the research. Anyone reading your abstract should be able to capture from those few sentences the essence of your research – what the research is about and how you intend to achieve its objectives. Abstract writing is an acquired skill and is likely take a number of drafts. To get an idea of what a good abstract looks like, check out the abstracts of articles in high-ranking journals within your discipline.

Introduction

The introduction is designed to set the scene for your research and to provide a rationale for the study. It lets the reader know something about the topic and what has already been discovered about it, and why you are interested in pursuing it further. An identification of the problem or issue under investigation is supported by background information that makes it possible for the reader to see why the specific topic was chosen and why the study needs to be undertaken. You might want to locate yourself within the study by clarifying your personal background and knowledge, and any preliminary studies you might have undertaken in relation to this study. You tell the reader why this research is important, why it needs to be undertaken, what contribution it will make to the field of knowledge, and in broad terms, what the wider implications might be.

Aims and objectives

From the introduction you lead into a clear statement of the purpose of the study: your overall aim and the specific goals (or set of objectives) you expect to achieve. Typically proposals use bullet points to identify the objectives. You need to specify your objectives clearly; for example, 'to investigate...' or 'to compare...' and so on.

Research questions

You need to specify your central guiding research question. The research question will identify the overall focus of the study. It needs to be clearly articulated, well-defined and significant. Sub-questions break the central questions down into manageable parts that will be addressed directly in the study. If your study uses a quantitative design, such as a causal-comparative or correlational study, you will provide a statement of your research hypothesis.

Conceptual framework and theory

Any study requires boundaries to be set. You need to show that you have thought about the boundaries by clarifying how you will respond to the research question. Typically, your thinking is given expression through your conceptual framework. You might choose a linear approach and list the themes, or you might provide a chart to illustrate the concepts and the relationships that you will be investigating. At this point you might want to make explicit the key terms, expressions, concepts or variables that are used in your study, and you will want to make clear to readers which particular definitions of these terms will be drawn upon.

Your study is likely to be anchored within a theoretical framework and underpinned by particular philosophical assumptions. The theory or theories you find appropriate to the kind of work you plan need to be discussed and their use in your study justified. Your study may be grounded in an existing theory, but if it is focused more on theory development, then you need to clarify that this is the role that theory will play in your study.

Literature review

The literature review serves an important function. It reports on what is known in your area by focusing on what has been done previously, and is intended to highlight similarities, shortfalls and any inconsistencies within the current knowledge base. It will reveal that there is an opening for your proposed study within that knowledge base. The literature review will demonstrate to the reader that your reading is relevant, up-to-date, and well-chosen to align with your own work. A good review will demonstrate that you are capable of contributing to this body of work.

If you have followed the chapters in this book in sequence, you will already have written your first draft of the literature review. It will be an extensive discussion of what has been found already on your topic, leading to a persuasive argument for your own research. Invariably your prepared review will be too long and detailed for full inclusion in the proposal. When your supervisor or advisor requests that it be shortened and sharpened for the proposal, they are not dismissing the time and effort involved in the original review. They are simply advising that a literature review in a proposal needs to sacrifice detail for evidence of your overall command of the topic in the context of previous and, often, seminal inquiries.

Methodology

The purpose of the methodology section is to describe what you plan to do in your study. It will clarify the research design and establish whether the study is, for example, ethnographic, action research or case study, and so forth. It will describe what tools you will use to gather data and who will take part in the study. It will discuss the methodological literature in relation to your research focus and the criteria you employed to make your methodological decisions. Your discussion will provide a justification that your methods are feasible and appropriate for answering your research question.

In this section you need to be extremely clear on what is going to happen during your research. Be explicit about where your study will take place, when it is going to happen, and how you will gain access to the site. Describe who is going to be involved, as well as why and how you will select and recruit those people. You also need to state the means by which you are going to gather the data. Will you interview, observe, survey, test, gather documentation, use photographs or records, or will you collect your data by other means? How will you record the information? Are you planning to use a questionnaire or interview schedule? Are you planning to analyze your data by themes? Will statistical analyses be involved?

Significance

You will have some idea, based on previous research, as to the sorts of outcomes you expect from your study. Your proposal needs to say why these outcomes might be significant contributions to, for example, policy, the profession, and the like. You will want to outline how your study advances knowledge and extends understandings provided in the literature of the area under investigation. Postgraduate researchers sometimes exaggerate the importance of their proposed study. Remember that you will be making a small contribution to knowledge, rather than one that is earth shattering.

Limitations

Any research finding is limited to the study at hand. Experienced research-ers openly discuss the ways in which the design and the specific conditions within it created limitations. You might want to discuss how your sample, the specific research site, the particular questions you asked, your (limited) access to documents, and so forth, imposed a number of constraints on the study. The reader should have a clear sense of your awareness that your findings cannot speak for everyone, in every context and for every time, but that your findings will still have credibility.

In order to make a start on the development of the proposal it is useful to write brief notes relating to your own research, for the sections we have just discussed.

Activity

RESEARCH PROPOSAL ORGANIZER

Copy the table, allowing for more space where needed to complete brief notes for each entry.

Key aspects	Key aspects related to my study
Central aim	
Research questions	
Important literature	
Conceptual framework	
Research design	
Data collection	
Data analysis methods	
Significance	
Limitations	

Ethical statements

Your university's Code of Ethical Conduct for research involving human sub-jects will guide your study. You must be able to assure the people assessing your proposal that you understand the importance of ethical behaviour in the production of knowledge and that you have addressed issues relating to the participants in your study. In particular, you will need to demonstrate that you are taking responsibility for protecting the confidentiality, anonymity and the physical and mental well-being of the participants in your research.

One way to begin your consideration is to reflect on who and what might be affected, both directly and indirectly, by your research. Think in terms of individuals, communities, present and future society, and so on. Decisions surrounding the recruitment of participants are made on the grounds of their relationship to your research questions. Once selected you need to provide participants with full details of the research so that they are able to provide free (and not coerced) consent with regard to the information provided. If you have identified likely harm to your participants, you need to give serious consideration to formulating new research questions and a new research design.

The timeline

Your proposal should include a timeline for your project, listing the times and dates for each step of your research process. A timeline demonstrates that you have given full attention to how you are going to manage and allocate time to all the activities. From the timeline the committee assessing your proposal will be able to determine whether or not your plan is realistic and whether or not it aligns with the timeframes provided for your research qualification. The timeline may take the form of a simple list of activities and an acknowledgment of the time allocated to each, or it may take the form of a diagram.

References

The purpose of the references is to acknowledge the ideas of others which you have drawn upon in your proposal. Your proposal should identify only the texts cited and should reflect the style preferred by your discipline. You should demonstrate consistency in the writing of the references. In addition, your university may require you to provide, as part of your proposal, a set of key references that will be central to your research.

Appendices (e.g., budget, instruments, resources etc.)

The appendices consist of any useful additional material. Include any research protocols, for example, the participants' information letter and consent form, a questionnaire, or the planned interview questions. Each new

Case Study 6.1

PROJECT TIMELINE

Philippa planned a three-year project to investigate digital technology use amongst children and young people. Her sites of interest centred on the home and extended to sport and leisure environments. Phase One of the project comprised a large-scale survey of children and young people. Phase Two was planned around interviews with selected children and young people and their parents on two different occasions. She prepared a timeline for her project as follows:

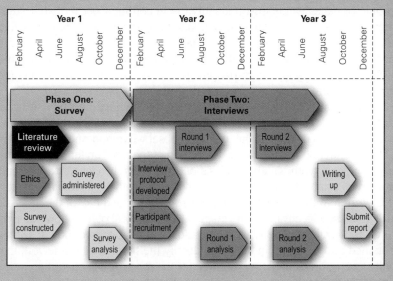

protocol is labelled as a new appendix. The Appendices might also include a budget in which you have estimated any financial costs. You may need to identify any resources necessary for you to conduct your study. For example, you may need to travel to your research site and you may need accommodation when you get there. You may need printing, stationery, postage for your survey, observation sheets or assessment instrument. You may need professional assistance with transcriptions of interviews (Oliver, Serovich and Mason, 2005). You may need to purchase a digital recorder or small video camera for recording your data. All these practicalities need to be considered.

Writing the research proposal

If you have worked through the earlier chapters in this book, you will have already given considerable thought to the key elements related to your study.

You will have made decisions on your topic and formulated your research questions. You will have produced a first draft of your literature review and you will have framed the design of your study. You will know who you want as participants in your research, where you will conduct your research, and by what means you will access and analyze your data (Punch, 2005).

The next stage is to transform these ideas into a discussion. We will begin with a written discussion of no more than two pages. Set aside one page for what your research is trying to find out and for setting out the background, and allow one page for how you plan to carry out your research. Writing a couple of pages will help you identify the important aspects of your study that you need to convey to others. In addition, you might want to talk to a friend (particularly someone unfamiliar with your topic area) about your proposed research. What is especially helpful about both these approaches is that they force you to confront precisely what, why and how you plan to do your research.

Notice that your written discussion is easily divided into two sections: (i) the introductory information and (ii) the research design. This is a guide for your proposal. The first half of the proposal will report on the first stages of the research. It will provide a description of the topic under investigation. It will offer a synthesis and analysis of past research relevant to the topic and it will establish a need for the study by noting the gaps in earlier work. It is written in the present and past tenses. The second half of the proposal will focus specifically on what you plan to do and will outline how you plan to do it. It will describe what information will be gathered, how it will be obtained and from whom, and will identify the theoretical framework that will serve as an explanatory resource for the study. It will be written in the future tense.

Now that you have written two pages and possibly talked to others about your proposed research, you need to expand on your written material and spoken ideas to develop a convincing case for your plan. Using the headings described above will make it easier. Subheadings might also be used to lend support to further detail within a section. You should adopt a style that is not overly formal but one that creates an engaging discussion. If possible, check out the style in which recent successful proposals in your discipline have been written and identify a style with which you feel comfortable.

The thing to know is that proposal writing takes time. In fact it will probably take you through more drafts than you anticipated. Allow more time than you think will be necessary so that the final document will be completed in good time. Ultimately you will want your proposal to be assessed as well-constructed, well-argued, reasoned and factually correct. You want it to demonstrate a logical consistency between its various elements so that you can convey to others that you have the argumentative and analytical skills required to make a contribution to knowledge.

Careless, loose and apologetic writing, overly long sentences, bad spelling, over-quoting, unnecessary repetition and jargon, and over-use of acronyms will not do you any favours. In fact, they may even label your research as a risk. Remember to conform to citation and referencing conventions. Since your readers may not be totally familiar with your field of study your proposal needs to be clear, concise and logical, as well as fully comprehensible to and sufficiently comprehensive for all readers. When you near completion of the final draft, put yourself in a reader's shoes and ask yourself if you feel that you know exactly what the proposed research is about, how it will be conducted, what will we all learn from it, and why it is worth doing. In your view, has any information been omitted that, if included, would make this proposal stronger? Is any information redundant? Would you, as a reader, be convinced that the research needs to proceed?

Defending the research proposal

Depending on the qualification you are working towards, your university may require you to defend your proposal orally to an approval panel or admissions board (Ruger, 2013). If the proposal is made clear and justifiable to the satisfaction of the panel or admissions board, you will be invited to proceed with your research. Since oral defence meetings are often formal occasions, you will need to be confident that you can explain and justify your plan, and then answer the panel's questions in order to convince them of the merits of the proposed research. Don't assume that the audience knows as much about the topic as you do. Equally, however, remember that the audience is an academic one, so pitch your presentation appropriately. In particular, you need to convince the panel that:

- The scope, quality and methods of the research you propose are likely to warrant award of your designated research qualification.
- The research as proposed is viable in terms of the word and time limits required of your research qualification.
- You have the necessary skills and knowledge to undertake the research.

The meeting will not only give you an opportunity to present information to an audience of varying expertise, experience and knowledge but, perhaps more importantly, it will also allow you to receive feedback on your proposed work. You may receive a positive endorsement for the way you plan to conduct the research, even before the research gets under way. Alternatively, the panel's differing viewpoints may alert you to aspects that you had overlooked. Use this feedback to your advantage to enhance your proposed study.

Many postgraduate researchers feel intimidated about this particular milestone, which requires them to speak with some authority about their planned research. Other postgraduate researchers seem to relish the opportunity. If you are one of the 'worriers' then here are a few suggestions:

- Be thoroughly prepared and try to anticipate the questions asked.
- Be positive and enthusiastic about what you are planning to research.
- Know your audience.
- Talk confidently and slowly.
- Use eye contact.
- Use pauses.
- Use technology, and visual and print aids purposefully.
- Conclude confidently.
- Practise before the event.

Liaise with your supervisor or advisor about the kinds of questions that the audience might ask you. When the time comes to deal with questions, listen carefully. If you do not understand the question, then ask for the questioner to repeat it. If you still do not know the answer, then say so. Be honest, rather than pretend to know. The important thing to remember about the defence of your research proposal is that you have to make a case for the study – you need to persuade the panel that this research should proceed. Don't try to impress with difficult terms and expressions; keep it simple and, above all, provide your audience with clarity. Perhaps the best advice is to attend proposal defences of other postgraduate researchers in your discipline at your university so that you can get a sense of what is expected and what the procedures are.

An important point to make at this stage is that the proposal is a working document. Although you may have convinced your defence panel that you have a clear sense of your topic and research question, and that you have a workable plan for the way you will collect and analyze the data, you need to be aware that the best made plans sometimes do not come to fruition. Although the proposal sets out a plan for what you intend to research, as well as how, why and when you will research it, you may well need to refine certain aspects as the research proceeds. You need to build a degree of flexibility into the plan to accommodate changes in the context and setting of the study so that you can make adjustments if things go wrong.

Ethics applications

The principles of research integrity and respect for persons during the undertaking of research will have been codified within your university. Codes of ethical and professional conduct for research have been developed by a number of different disciplines including psychology (American Psychological Association [APA]; British Psychological Society [BPS]), sociology (British Sociological Association [BSA]); education (American Educational Research Association [AERA]; British Educational Research Association (BERA); and anthropology (American Anthropological Association [AAA]). These professional ethical standards have been developed and adopted from an understanding of the rights and responsibilities of human beings in relation to the specific research undertaken within the discipline. The standards will also be informed by the 1949 Nuremberg Code, based on the principles of voluntary consent, the avoidance of harm, social good and ongoing risk analysis, and will be constructed around the point that it is indefensible to treat human beings as objects and as a means to the researcher's ends.

Activity

CODE OF ETHICAL CONDUCT

Search your institution's website, locating its code of ethical conduct for research with human participants.

1. Read the regulations and procedures carefully.
2. List the ethical concerns that apply to your project.
3. Consider the measures that could be put in place to ensure the ethical integrity of your project.
4. Download an application form from your institution's site.
5. Complete a first draft of the application form.

You will have noticed that completing the ethics application is a time-consuming process. It is quite likely that your first draft will not necessarily represent your final application. In fact, some committees may want to interview you or, at the very least, ask you to reflect again on the ethical implications of your application. If you have not allowed sufficient time for ethical clearance in the timetable you developed earlier in this chapter then you will need to make some amendments.

The ethical application focuses primarily on the link between your research methods and your participants. While you will need to explain the purpose of the research, the committee will be looking carefully at your plan for recruiting participants and for accessing the research site as well as your expectations of and proposed interactions with participants in the study. You will also probably be asked for any letters of information, consent forms or transcribers' agreements, all of which will provide a measure of the particular way you will deal with the needs and rights of participants and with the integrity of the project. Once approval has been received you will be able to begin the truly exciting component of the research – the work 'in the field'.

Review

Main points
- A research proposal is a central feature of all research activity.
- Proposals describe the intentions of the researcher and outline how the research will be undertaken.
- The proposal clarifies and justifies the aims, contextualized within the literature. It outlines the methodology, addresses limitations and ethical issues, and maps out a timeline.
- A proposal is written to convince others of the merit of your plan and also to convince others that you are capable of carrying out that plan.
- Some universities require that the proposal be defended orally.
- All research must comply with codes of ethical practice.
- Ethics applications address issues to do with research integrity and respect for persons.

Key Terms
- Research proposal
- Defence of the proposal
- Ethical approval

Looking ahead

This chapter brought us to the end of the stages from your very early thinking about your research to approval for you to proceed with your planned research. The next chapter looks briefly at what lies ahead in the research process. It explores the formal support that is available to you to make your research journey an enriching experience. It then looks at the examination process and explores how you might get your research known about and read by others once you have navigated your way through the journey.

7 Looking Ahead to the Next Steps

Planning flexibility

Now that you have successfully defended your research proposal, you can begin to put your plans into action. This is a truly exciting time. All those insecurities about your own capabilities and getting things right seem to disappear. You now have the official word that your research has merit and that others have confidence in your capacity to undertake the work. Once you have gained any necessary ethical clearance you can begin to prepare for the next stage of the process. Data collection is first on the list, and you start to think about what it will be like to be in the field or immersed in archives or working with others. And there is much to do. You may need to recruit participants and seek permission for a site to undertake your research. There may be video and audio recorders to organize. There may be transcribers to find and book.

The point to be aware of is that the excitement may quickly turn to a feeling that you are losing control of things. New research plans are open to change in response to, say, the availability of resources, research sites, and participants. You may encounter very real difficulties in analyzing and managing the data. There will be tedious times, lonely hours, setbacks and scary blocks. Although you might find this difficult to fathom, there will also be people who doubt what you are trying to do and people who have little faith in your ability to undertake this study. There will be others whose 'helpfulness' is not in any way helpful to your work. Along with the privilege of doing research, there's the responsibility – to your participants, to your supervisors, to the discipline – which from time to time might seem overwhelming.

So how do you prepare for unforeseen eventualities? Building a degree of flexibility into your plans will help accommodate changes in the context and setting of the study and will help you make adjustments when things go wrong. Of course, you will only be making changes when you have discussed all options with your supervisor or advisor and when modifications are deemed absolutely necessary. You should also consider running a pilot study to check out coverage and procedures on your questionnaire instrument. And you should trial your interview schedule, practise your interviewing skills and test out your recording equipment with a non-participant. Through the data collection phase, you need to be patient, committed and strong. You need to accommodate your participants' schedules, needs and expectations. Flexibility on your part will go a long way when you are confronted with unanticipated changes to systems or personnel within your research site. Coping with the highs and lows of the research process is part and parcel of the research journey. But, keep in mind that there will also be breakthrough moments when the loneliness, tedium and personal doubts are forgotten in the excitement of new insights.

Taking advantage of support

Your research is a shared responsibility. The university, at the overarching level, provides frameworks, policies, regulations and codes of conduct that set you up for success in your research programme. A number of individuals, for example, supervisors and advisors, will also be responsible for establishing processes and creating arrangements that contribute to your success. Your university will be very keen for you to succeed. It will ensure that efficient systems are in place to provide you with the infrastructural support you need and the human and material resources necessary for you to complete your research. Supervision, library resources, language support (for students who are not writing in their first language), seminars, workshops, on-line materials, handbooks, induction programmes, technological support and funding are just some of the ways in which your university will be supporting your research journey. You, of course, are the central player in this arrangement and you can maximize your chances of success by taking advantage of the support on offer. Taking advantage of the support does require certain responsibilities from you, just as it provides you with certain rights.

INSIGHTS FROM A POSTGRADUATE RESEARCHER

"You find support in a wide range of places. For me, working with an amazing group of research participants who made me think clearly about what I was doing certainly helped beyond expectation. I found that they tended to ask me questions that helped me to focus and that made me think outside the square for alternate solutions. This helped with both the research process and the final outcomes."

"It helps to have a strong support person at home."

As we noted in Chapter 3, the library is a repository of important resources for the successful completion of your study. Databases that host a wide range of literature allow you to search widely for relevant literature. In addition, within your specific discipline, the library will provide guides to selected information sources such as reference resources and websites. More importantly, perhaps, the library will offer you access to electronic and/or paper copies of the most recent articles from a range of journals, as well as access to many of the latest books, periodicals and reports relevant to your work. The library may provide an inter-library loan service for a small fee. Libraries invariably provide an on-line research tool to assist researchers with information and advice relating to aspects such as qualitative and quantitative research, research design, writing and literature reviews.

Your growth as a researcher is enhanced by the research culture at your university. There is a lot to be said for being around similarly minded people. Use their enthusiasm about new insights within the field and their methods of solving intellectual problems as a way of learning tacitly about the way in which academics think and act. Use it as support for the work you are doing, as an incentive for completing your next piece of work. Other postgraduate researchers will not necessarily be able to offer sound advice on writing and illuminating discussions on research, but they will provide a valuable means of support and a listening ear. Affirmation of what you are doing is important at all stages of the process, even when you are moving along confidently. Emotional support is particularly important when the writing is not progressing, when you have difficulties accessing the research site or participants, when the data do not seem to be supporting your hunches, and, in short, when any kind of problem blocks your way forward.

INSIGHTS FROM A POSTGRADUATE RESEARCHER

"The action research process is not easy to go through. There are many times when I doubt my capabilities and whether I should even attempt something that could impact on other people's practice. It would not be possible to do this in a workplace that was anything but positive and supportive."

However, the most influential form of support you receive during your research will almost certainly be provided by your supervisor or advisor. Your supervisor is the principal resource for your study, and because of that, getting a good match is extremely important. You may not have any say in the matter, in which case, you will find yourself assigned a staff member who will be responsible for guiding you through your study. You will require a supervision relationship that is effective and productive for you both to ensure that the research is completed on time and, importantly, to ensure that you grow intellectually. An effective supervision relationship, like any relationship, demands considerable effort and goodwill from both parties. It is a complex relationship because, on the one hand, you certainly do not want to be told what to do every step of the way, and would prefer to take charge of your research. Yet, on the other hand, you do not want to be left entirely to your own devices. You want balanced support that consists of sufficient care and attention to progress the project and to develop your skills and knowledge that will contribute to you becoming a professional researcher.

Case Study 7.1

KIERAN'S RESEARCH SUPERVISION

Kieran's research was based within the education department at his university. He planned a one-year study of his own teaching in a school and wanted to unpack the way in which he taught chemistry to senior secondary school students. His university was able to assign a supervisor with expertise in school chemistry and a supervisor with expertise in self-study. Since both supervisors got on well together and had Kieran's project's interests at heart, the supervision meetings, from Kieran's perspective, were collegial and instructive.

Your project completion is the overriding goal for the supervisor (Taylor, 2002). Not only must your supervisor establish support structures and enable interactions that are conducive to timely completion of the project and that contribute to an enriching experience for you, but he or she must ensure that standards are upheld to the satisfaction of doctoral stakeholders from the institution and the discipline. In order to carry out this multidimensional role, your supervisor provides an ethic of care that sits alongside an ethos of confidence in your capabilities, bringing to the arrangement a vast array of competencies: research expertise; an awareness of and compliance with expected standards; skills related to project management, editing, critique, mentoring and coaching; attributes to support and sponsor your project and to make it possible for you to grow intellectually; and personal skills and sensitivities that are responsive to your needs.

Supervisors operate with different styles and methods and they need to agree between themselves what will work best. You, too, will want to be clear in the negotiation process about what approaches you consider would work best for you. Are you someone who blossoms with minimal guidance, or are you someone who needs strong direction and detailed feedback? Until these differences are out in the open and negotiated, you could all find yourselves working towards different objectives. Projects that proceed successfully to completion do so without unnecessary confusion over expectations. Many universities require supervisors and postgraduate researchers to formalize working arrangements through a written contract. Even if your university does not require a contractual arrangement, it is always useful to draw up a statement of expectations. When you and your supervisors comply with the terms of your working relationship, as outlined in your statement of expectations, things are more likely to proceed smoothly.

While you need to demonstrate consistent effort throughout the entire project, keep in mind that your supervisors' involvement will be more intensive during some stages of the project. As the nature of the work changes over the course of the project, and as your maturity as a researcher develops, the nature of the supervision relationship is likely to change. At all stages, however, it is important that you maintain your working relationship, even if it is simply to keep your supervisors informed of what you are doing in your project. At supervision meetings, honouring your side of the bargain means that you will need to take care that your involvement in the relationship remains at all times at the professional level. Your professional responsibilities in the supervision relationship require you to be punctual for meetings and to be well prepared. Supervisors are permitted to be late but you are not.

Good preparation is important if you hope to negotiate your move from dependent learner to independent researcher. Be sure that you have completed the objectives you set out for the meeting and provide your supervisors with a brief written account of how you met those objectives. Give your supervisors plenty of time to read the progress report and any other written work before the set meeting. At the meeting tell the supervisors in your own words how you are progressing and the small breakthroughs you have made. Let them also know of any issues you encountered and tell them what you have done to resolve those issues. Your supervisors will appreciate honesty and are fully aware that research is often uncertain and ambiguous. They will particularly want to know how issues have been resolved. If solutions have not been forthcoming through your own efforts, then ask for specific advice and guidance.

When supervision sessions advance the research through discussion and debate of complex ideas, the experience is often an exhilarating one for all involved. Unlike your previous experiences of teaching and learning structures in which you listened, watched and learned, the supervision meeting is more collegial and more balanced in participant contribution. You and your supervisors all learn from the academically 'charged' thinking that is shared and from the collaborative explorations that take place. Establishing an environment that explores a range of ideas may not, however, come easily to your supervisors. It may require a level of creativity on your part which, in turn, you can offer by putting both well-conceived and underdeveloped ideas forward as a starting point for discussion at the meeting. Like most things in life, you will derive more satisfaction from the supervision meetings when you contribute more effort.

The examination process

We are now going to look way ahead to the time when you are about to submit your research for examination. Your supervisors have indicated that they are satisfied that the work is ready to be examined. If you are undertaking research at the masters or doctoral levels then your work will shortly be on its way to the examiners. After a long period of perseverance, ups and downs, and above all, genuine hard work on your part, you are finally on the home stretch to becoming a researcher in your chosen field. It is likely that your written thesis or research report will be the principal means by which you are identified as a competent researcher in the examiners' written reports.

It is important that you are fully aware of the procedures and processes within your university regarding the examination. In many universities, the names of potential examiners will be considered by your supervisors and possibly the Head of the Department. Once examiners are decided upon, and availability is confirmed, their names are passed on to the institution. In many respects it will be helpful if you know the identity of your examiners and to have this information well before your work is submitted. It's helpful because if you have not made reference to their publications in appropriate and relevant places within the work, then you will have the opportunity to do so before the work is completed. Citing, quoting and discussing the work of your examiners in a way that enriches your work is always a good strategy.

It is likely that your work will be assessed by two or three examiners. One may be based within your own university, while the others are likely to be external to your university. Most examiners will have expertise and experience, usually within an applied field relevant to your work, at a level deemed appropriate for assessing your research. Examiners will be involved in the wider area in which your research is situated. None of the examiners will have been involved in supervising your work. Nor should they have acted as an advisor in any capacity during the development of the thesis or worked with you in any other research project.

Shortly after you submit your work the examiners will receive a hard copy of your work. Along with the work the university will provide advice on the examination procedures and on the format expected of the examination report. The examiners are asked to provide a report which is reflective of their own views and which is not produced following consultation with anyone else. The report will usually note any changes that the examiner considers *mandatory* for an acceptable standard. The report will also note any *recommended* changes. Examiners will be asked to make an overall assessment recommendation on the basis of their reading of the thesis.

If the mere mention of the word 'examination' makes you anxious, then take heart. Examiners, at the outset, do not entertain a view of you as an intruder, seeking uninvited entry into the researcher community. They do not look negatively upon your scholarly ambitions and, hence, they do not expect that you will fail. Since their work will be related in some way to yours, they anticipate that engaging with your work will be an illuminating and uplifting experience. While this may sound strange to you right now, they will also be hoping to learn from your work. The fact that they will be happy to spend a large portion of their time giving thoughtful consideration to your work should be a source of reassurance to you. In return, they expect you will have something important to say and that your findings will shed new light on the field in which they, like you, are immersed.

Very few people are likely to engage with your work to the same extent that your examiners do. Even if their viewpoint does not match yours entirely, they will do their best to get 'on the same page'. Be aware that they will not necessarily engage with your work in the logical progression that you present to them. All readers get a grip of written content in different ways. If you can't assume that your reader will progress through in the order your chapters are presented, then you will need to be absolutely sure that there is a logical coherence and a strong consistency throughout the work. If you communicate your ideas clearly and compellingly and created a sense of fascination and wonder through your argument, then your examiner will find your work difficult to put down.

Examiners' reports are usually a few pages long, but just as a short report is not an indicator of exemplary work, a long report will not indicate that your work is marginal. Some reports will follow the format preferred by the university and some may follow the chapter headings. Some may follow the conventions of the discipline, while others will take their own trajectory. Whatever the format, all reports will make a number of observations that, taken together, will assess the suitability of the thesis for the award of the appropriate qualification. By now you should be quite familiar with what they will be looking for, so, in brief to remind you, the observations they make will be related to:

- The comprehensiveness of the study and its contribution to knowledge.
- Your familiarity with and understanding of the relevant literature.
- The articulation of the research questions.
- The identification of research methods, their justification and application.
- The honest reporting of the findings.
- The careful analysis of the findings and their relevance within the wider context of knowledge.
- The quality of the written language and general presentation.

Examiners expect to read a logical and coherent argument presented with attention to grammar and free from typographical errors. If there is one thing that is guaranteed to get your examiner off-side right from the beginning it is work that is full of spelling mistakes, grammatical errors and issues with graphs and statistical analysis. Under no circumstances should you submit a half-baked or borderline report, thesis or dissertation with the expectation that your examiners will strengthen your weak draft by pointing out the errors of your ways and salvage the thesis for you.

What the examiners are particularly looking for is your ability to undertake research. They are also looking for intellectual depth and rigour, and a demonstration of your independence as a researcher. They will be searching for virtually flawless presentation and evidence of a sound methodology, as well as a range of abilities including creative skills, higher level thinking skills and analytical skills. Most of all, the examiners will be looking for the X-factor in your work and your point of difference from other work. They want to be able to assess the work as a piece of research that commands respect within the field.

INSIGHTS FROM A POSTGRADUATE RESEARCHER

"While the journey to the top of the mountain is full of hidden crevasses and vertical cliff faces, it is possible to get there no matter what your experience in mountain climbing/research is. When you get there, stop and look around. The view from the mountain top is great!"

Looking beyond completion

Looking way ahead to the time when you have completed and passed your research paper, plan some time to enjoy the activities that were not possible during your research journey. You might plan a well-earned holiday. Many postgraduate researchers experience mixed emotions at the completion of a research project, ranging from a feeling of being at a loose end, a huge sense of relief and a lack of motivation. Don't be surprised at these feelings, but try not to let them take charge. One suggestion is to move on to a new project and, quite frankly, there is no better project than to share your new-found knowledge with others. Interestingly, very few research theses and dissertations are read thoroughly by anyone other than the supervisors and examiners. After all the time and effort you have given to your topic area it does not make a lot of sense to let your contribution gather dust on a shelf. Others will want to be made aware of your new ideas, your innovative analyses and your findings. Let them know how your new knowledge supports or challenges the literature and, in that capacity, how it advances the discipline and empowers the profession. Don't hesitate in getting your work out there.

It is likely that your new knowledge will be of interest to your professional community, the policy arena or the commercial field. You might seek publication in academic journals (Murray, 2013) to share your new knowledge with your fellow researchers since your work will be publishable in part, at least (Thomson and Kamler, 2013). However, you might be more attracted to reporting your work in non-refereed publications of professional associations and in conference proceedings. You might also be highly interested in reporting on your work through newspapers, magazines and internet blogs, as well as by speaking on television and radio in order to gain a wider social outreach and generate interest in your specific topic area. Presentations to practitioners and policy-makers might also appeal.

Whatever your professional destination, you need others to read and hear what you have to say. Getting your work 'out there' to a wider audience is the primary means by which you are able to have an influence on the thinking within your discipline. However, that involves planning. It requires you to establish a personal programme of writing and regular protected writing time to accomplish your publication plans. Consider the different aspects of your work and figure out how each of the aspects that you want to share with others could be constructed to offer new knowledge. It is quite likely that you will be able to see how the discipline, the profession and policy makers could all benefit from your new knowledge in different ways.

Getting your work 'out there' will require you to think creatively in order to find a space in the current academic, professional and policy conversations for you to make a contribution. Being flexible and making connections will allow you to add to the current conversation. No-one in the research community wants the current conversation completely stifled by a newcomer. Your particular 'take' has to be both compatible with and respectful of the investment that the research community has already made in the conversation. What the community will be particularly interested in is reading and hearing the issues and questions that concern them most being addressed in new ways.

Presentations to the academic, professional, practitioner and policy communities, to industry and commercial representatives and to the general public through the media, are all certain ways of getting your work 'out there'. Obviously, given the conference registration and travel costs, you will need to be selective and identify the conference(s) that most closely align with your research interests. The great thing about conference attendance is the chance to form long-term networks, associations and potential collaborations, as well as sharing your ideas, your findings and your new knowledge face-to-face with scholars who have common points of interest with your research. Take the opportunity, because, as a newcomer to the academic conference scene, building networks and friendships will be hugely influential in the development of your career.

You will need to plan ahead simply because abstracts or proposals from presenters are required long before the academic conference date. Check out the conference website for information about timelines and requirements. Pay particular attention to the time allocated for the presentation and the technology provided to assist in your Microsoft® PowerPoint presentation. Find out whether or not you are required to submit a paper in addition to the abstract, and if so, when and whether it will be peer-reviewed. While the headings for the paper will be much the same as those required for a journal article, you will find that it is considerably easier to get acceptance for a paper published in conference proceedings than it is for a paper in a journal.

The presentation itself is designed for audience engagement. Speak confidently and slowly, especially if your conference includes international attendees who may struggle with the language. Offer the background details if you consider them important for understanding what you did and what you found. Remember, you want the audience to engage with your presentation so do not take them through unnecessary material. Your presentation should note a few key points and the best always offer a 'take home' message. Anticipate and prepare for questions from the audience and use any issues raised during the discussion following your presentation to strengthen any unfinished writing.

There are likely to be other presentations that you want to make to specific groups within the profession and within the community. While you won't need to provide a paper for those situations, the same principles apply to the actual presentation. Essentially, you want to engage your audience so that you can share your knowledge and so that you can generate discussion. The media might hold attraction for you as a means of communicating your work. However, fronting up to the media successfully is, more often than not, a learned skill. Seek assistance about how you can create a story about your work in a way that captures the interest of the listener or the viewer.

Some academic conferences include poster sessions. These sessions are also a useful forum for promoting your work. In many ways the sessions are less daunting because you don't have to confront an audience who may want to debate your ideas vigorously. You are spared the task of a formal presentation and you get the opportunity to talk with like-minded individuals and small groups. Essentially, you are given a time-slot to showcase your poster of a pre-determined size and/or a display on your laptop. The poster you have prepared will be attractively designed with the main features and key findings from your study which you will be able to explain in more detail if required.

Final words

This brings us to the very last section of the book. By now you will be fully aware that research is an orderly process. It involves steps that, when taken sequentially and with careful consideration, will develop your research skills and understandings and, more importantly, will point you along the path of success. You will know what is required to complete your research on time and successfully.

By reading this book, you will have discovered that research is not a total mystery but that it is actually a reasonably coherent process. We have covered a great deal of ground, which has included:

- Meeting new terminology.
- Learning about ethical research and how to formulate a good research question.
- Exploring conceptual frameworks.
- Discovering the importance of the literature, where to access sources that are relevant to the research, and the secrets of writing a good literature review.
- Looking at a number of research designs and exploring their different purposes.
- Learning about methods to gather and analyze data in order to answer a specific research question.
- Considering what needs to be discussed in a research proposal and how to make the proposal acceptable.
- Looking ahead to the time beyond the proposal stage, towards the high tension of working in the field and the support on offer, to the examination stage, and, finally, to disseminating your findings.

It is now time to wish you all the best as you make your way through the research planning steps ahead.

Review

Main points

- Research does not always go according to plan. Building in flexibility is important.
- Your university, the library, your colleagues and peers provide you with support for you to succeed.
- The most influential form of support will almost certainly be provided by your supervisor.
- Examiners anticipate that they will learn more about your topic as a result of reading your work.
- Examiners each provide an independent written report on your work.
- Your work needs to be put out in the research, professional, or policy communities.
- Presentations to a range of different communities are a helpful way for you to disseminate your findings.

Key Terms

- Institutional policies, regulations and codes of conduct for research
- Supervision
- Examination process
- Dissemination of findings

References

Adler, P.A. and Adler, P. (1994) 'Observational techniques', in N.K. Denzin and Y.S. Lincoln (eds), *Handbook of Qualitative Research* (pp. 126–185). London: Sage.

Bernath, U. and Vidal, M. (2007) 'The theories and the theorists: Why theory is important for research', *Distances et savoirs*, 5(3), 427–458. Retrieved from www.eden-online.org/contents/conferences/research/barcelona/D_S-Holmberg-Moore-Peters-Oct06.pdf

Bochner, A.P. and Ellis, C. (2002) *Ethnographically Speaking: Autoethnography, literature and aesthetics.* Oxford: Alta Mira Press.

Burton, S. and Steane, P. (eds) (2005) *Surviving Your Thesis.* London: Routledge.

Carr, W. and Kemmis, S. (1986) *Becoming Critical: Education, knowledge and action research.* London: Falmer Press.

Carter, S., Kelly, F. and Brailsford, I. (2012) *Structuring your Research Thesis.* Basingstoke: Palgrave Macmillan.

Casey, A. (2012) 'A self-study using action research: changing site expectations and practice stereotypes', *Educational Action Research*, 20(2), 219–232.

Castello, M., Inesta, A. and Monereo, C. (2009) 'Towards self-regulated academic writing: an exploratory study with graduate students in a situated learning environment', *Electronic Journal of Research in Educational Psychology*, 7(3), 1107–1130.

Charmaz, K. (2003) 'Grounded theory: objectivist and constructivist methods', in N.K. Denzin and Y.S. Lincoln (eds) *Collecting and Interpreting Qualitative Materials.* Thousand Oaks, CA: Sage.

Cohen, L., Manion, L. and Morrison, K. (2007) *Research Methods in Education*, 6th edn. London and New York: Routledge.

Costa, A.L. and Kallick, B. (1993) 'Through the lens of a critical friend', *Educational Leadership*, 51(2), 49.

Craswell, G. (2005) *Writing For Academic Success. A postgraduate guide.* London: Sage.

Cresswell, J.W. (2009) *Research Design: Qualitative, quantitative and mixed method approaches*, 3rd edn. Thousand Oaks, CA: Sage.

Crotty, M. (1998) *The Foundations of Social Research: Meaning and perspective in the research process.* Crows Nest, NSW: Allen & Unwin.

Denscombe, M. (2003) *The Good Research Guide for Small-scale Social Research Projects*, 2nd edn. Maidenhead: Open University Press.

Denzin, N.K. and Lincoln, Y.S. (eds) (2008) *The Landscape of Qualitative Research*, 3rd edn. Thousand Oaks, CA: Sage.

Ellis, C.S. and Bochner, A. (2000) 'Autoethnography, personal narrative, reflexivity: researcher as subject', in N.K. Denzin and Y.S. Lincoln (eds) *Handbook of Qualitative Research*, 2nd edn (pp. 733–768). Thousand Oaks, CA: Sage.

Felton, S. (2008) 'Why do a postgraduate research degree?', in G. Hall and J. Longman (eds) *The Postgraduate's Companion.* London: Sage.

Fink, A. (2005) *Conducting Research Literature Reviews: From internet to paper*, 2nd edn. London: Routledge Falmer.

Flores, E. and Nerad, M. (2012) 'Peers in doctoral education: unrecognized partners', *New Directions for Higher Education*, 157, 73–83.

Fraenkel, J.R. and Wallen, N.E. (2008) *How to Design and Evaluate Research in Education*, 7th edn. New York: McGraw-Hill.

Gillham, B. (2000) *The Research Interview*. London: Continuum.

Gray, D.E. (2004) *Doing Research in the Real World*. London: Sage.

Green, P. and Usher, R. (2003) 'Fast supervision: Changing supervisory practice in changing times', *Studies in Continuing Education*, 25(1), 37–50.

Guba, E. and Lincoln, Y. S. (1985) *Naturalistic Inquiry*. Beverley Hills: Sage.

Holly, M.L.H. (1997) *Keeping a Professional Journal*, 2nd edn. Malvern, Vic.: Deakin University Press.

Howell, M. and Prevenier, W. (2001) *From Reliable Sources: An introduction to historical research*. Ithaca, NY: Cornell Universty Press.

Hughes, S., Pennington, J.L. and Makris, S. (2012) 'Translating autoethnography across the AERA Standards: toward understanding autoethnographic scholarship as empirical research', *Educational Researcher*, 41(6), 209–219.

Hurst, B., Wilson, C. and Cramer, G. (1998) 'Professional teaching portfolios', *Phi Delta Kappan*, 79(8), 578.

Ingleton, C. and Cadman, K. (2002) 'Silent issues for international postgraduate research students: emotion and agency in academic success', *Australian Educational Researcher*, 29(1), 93–113.

Jones, E. (2001) 'Portfolio assessment as a means of professional development', *New Zealand Annual Review of Education*, 10, 187–202

Kamler, B. and Thomson, P. (2006) *Helping Doctoral Students Write: Pedagogies for supervision*. London: Routledge.

King, N. and Horrocks, C. (2010) *Interviews in Qualitative Research*. London: Sage.

Lantolf, J.P. (2004) 'Introducing sociocultural theory', in J.P. Lantolf (ed.) *Sociocultural Theory and Second Language Learning* (pp. 1–26). Oxford: Oxford University Press.

Leshem, S. and Trafford, V. (2007) 'Overlooking the conceptual framework', *Innovations in Education and Teaching International*, 44(1), 93–105.

Maxwell, J.A. and Loomis, D.M. (2003) 'Mixed method design: an alternative approach', in A. Tashakkori and C. Teddlie (eds) *Handbook of Mixed Methods in Social and Behavioral Research* (pp. 241–272). Thousand Oaks, CA: Sage.

McMillan, K. and Weyers, J. (2013) *How to Write and Research a Successful PhD*. London: Pearson.

Menard, S. (1991) *Longitudinal Research*. Thousand Oaks, CA: Sage.

Mertens, D.M. (2005) *Research and Evaluation in Education and Psychology: Integrating diversity with quantitative, qualitative, and mixed methods*, 2nd edn. Thousand Oaks, CA: Sage.

Morgan, D.L. (1997) *Focus Groups as Qualitative Research*. Thousand Oaks, CA: Sage.

Morse, J.M. (2005) 'Principles of mixed methods and multimethod research design', in A. Tashakkori and C.K.F. Punch (eds) *Introduction to Social Research: Quantitative and qualitative approaches*, 2nd edn. London: Sage.

Murray, R. (2013) *Writing for Academic Journals*, 3rd edn. Maidenhead, McGraw-Hill International.

Oliver, D.G., Serovich, J.M. and Mason, T.L. (2005) 'Constraints and opportunities with interview transcription: towards reflection in qualitative research', *Social Forces*, 84(2), 1273–1289.

Ortlipp, M. (2008) 'Keeping and using reflective journals in the qualitative research process', *The Qualitative Report*, 13(4), 695–705.

Patton, M.Q. (2002) *Qualitative Research & Evaluation Methods*, 3rd edn. Thousand Oaks, CA: Sage.

Pears, R. and Shields, G. (2008) *Cite Them Right: The essential referencing guide*, 8th edn. Basingstoke: Palgrave Macmillan.

Potter, J. and Wetherell, M. (1987) *Discourse and Social Psychology*. Thousand Oaks, CA: Sage.

Punch, K.L. (2005) *Developing Effective Research Proposals*, 2nd edn. London: Sage.

Rosier, M.J. (1988) 'Survey research methods', in J.P. Keeves (ed.) *Educational Research, Methodology, and Measurement*. Oxford: Pergamon Press.

Ruger, S. (2013) *How to Write a Good PhD Thesis and Survive the Viva*. Milton Keynes: Open University.

Scott, D. and Usher, R. (2003) *Researching Education: Data, methods and theory in educational enquiry*. London: Continuum.

Seidman, I. (2006) *Interviewing as Qualitative Research: A guide for researchers in education and the social sciences*, 3rd edn. New York: Teachers College Press.

Shadish, W.R., Cook, T.D. and Campbell, D.T. (2002) *Experimental and Quasi-experimental Designs for Generalized Causal Inference*. Boston: Houghton Mifflin.

Somekh, B. (2006) *Action Research: A methodology for change and development*. Maidenhead: Open University Press.

Taylor, S. (2002) 'Managing postgraduate research degrees', in S. Ketteridge, S. Marshall and H. Fry (eds) *The Effective Academic: A handbook for enhanced academic practice* (pp. 131–147). London: Kogan Page.

Thomson, P. and Kamler, B. (2013) *Writing for Peer Reviewed Journals: Strategies for getting published*. London: Routledge.

Walshaw, M. (2007) *Working with Foucault in Education*. Rotterdam: Sense Publishers.

Willig, C. (2012) *Qualitative Interpretation and Analysis in Psychology*. Maidenhead: McGraw-Hill/Open University Press.

Wisker, G. (2007) *The Postgraduate Research Handbook: Succeed with your MA, MPhil, EdD and PhD*. Basingstoke: Palgrave Macmillan.

Yin, R.K. (2003) *Case Study Research: Design and methods* (Vol. 5) Thousand Oaks, CA: Sage.

Yin, R.K. (2011) *Qualitative Research from Start to Finish*. New York: Guilford Press.

Further Reading

Benn, K. and Benn, C. (2006) *Professional Thesis Presentation: A step-by-step guide to preparing your thesis in Microsoft Word*. Auckland: Pearson Prentice Hall.

Carter, S., Kelly, F. and Brailsford, I. (2012) *Structuring Your Research Thesis*. Basingstoke: Palgrave Macmillan.

Corbin, J. and Strauss, A. (2008) *Basics of Qualitative Research*, 3rd edn. Thousand Oaks, CA: Sage.

Cresswell, J.W. (2009) *Research Design: Qualitative, quantitative and mixed method approaches*, 3rd edn. Thousand Oaks, CA: Sage.

Denscombe, M. (2003) *The Good Research Guide for Small-scale Social Research Projects*, 2nd edn. Maidenhead: Open University Press.

Pears, R. and Shields, G. (2008) *Cite Them Right: The essential referencing guide*, 8th edn. Basingstoke: Palgrave Macmillan.

Punch, K.L. (2005) *Developing Effective Research Proposals*, 2nd edn. London: Sage.

Walshaw, M. (2012) *Getting to Grips with Doctoral Research*. Basingstoke: Palgrave Macmillan.

Wisker, G. (2007) *The Postgraduate Research Handbook: Succeed with your MA, MPhil, EdD and PhD*. Basingstoke: Palgrave Macmillan.

Wisker, G. (2012) *The Good Supervisor*, 2nd edn. Basingstoke: Palgrave Macmillan.

Yin, R.K. (2011) *Qualitative Research from Start to Finish*. New York: Guilford Press.

Glossary

Action research: a collaborative research design that begins with a problem or an issue within a setting and involves the people within the setting working through a process to bring about a change.

Analysis: the interpretation and presentation of data, typically through theory and drawing on the literature, with the purpose of developing a clearer understanding.

Anonymity: the unknown identity of a participant, arranged for ethical reasons.

Case study: a research design, often using a range of data sources to focus in-depth attention on a 'case' – one individual, one group, one setting, an activity or an issue – or to focus on multiple cases.

Citation: a reference in the text to specific research, identifying the author and year of the published research, using either a direct quote or by a précis of an aspect of the research.

Coding: organizing the data through categories, labels or themes.

Conceptual framework: an organization, often displayed in diagrammatic or narrative form, of the concepts and their interrelationships that are important to your research.

Concepts: the ideas or phenomena that are central to your research.

Confidentiality: the protection of a research participant's identity for ethical reasons.

Content analysis: an interpretation of the content in the data, such as in documents, by looking for themes, patterns or trends.

Convenience sample: a sample from the population, comprising participants who can be accessed easily and conveniently.

Correlation: the relationship between one variable and another.

Data: the sets of information that you will collect to provide an answer to your research questions.

Empirical research: research that depends on the collection of data sources or evidence to substantiate the claims made.

Epistemology: a theory of knowledge that responds to questions concerning the nature of knowledge and the development and creation of knowledge.

Ethics: employing standards and taking the morally right course of action in research activity, avoiding conflicts of interests and adverse effect.

Ethnography: a research design that requires the researcher's direct involvement with a group in its natural setting and is focused on understanding their dynamic cultural world.

Experiment: a research design that is used to investigate the effect of an intervention, and explores what happens when one variable is systematically manipulated over another variable.

Fieldwork: the work that the researcher does to collect data in a setting.

Focus group: a data collection method of a group interview, aimed at eliciting a wide range of views, to gain greater insight from the group's interaction than might be possible through individual interviewing.

Grounded theory: a research design that draws on the perceptions of people in order to generate an explanatory theory that might explain what is going on in a holistic way.

Hypothesis: a theory, idea or educated guess in the form of a statement to be tested then accepted or rejected after data collection by the researcher.

Informed consent: verbal or written confirmation from participants that provides assurance that they have been informed of the purpose of and their involvement and rights within the research.

Interpretivism: a paradigm focused on unearthing participants' understandings of their experiences.

Interview: a data collection method that seeks to gain an in-depth understanding of the human phenomena being studied, conducted with individuals or with focus groups of people and consisting of structured, unstructured or semi-structured formats.

Interview schedule: a set of questions developed particularly for a structured or semi-structured interview to explore the response of an individual or a group to the phenomena being studied.

Instruments: tools that assist in the data collection, such as interview schedules questionnaires and observation sheets.

Life history: a research design that is focused on the personal experiences and lifestyles of individuals or groups over a period of time.

Literature review: a summary and critical commentary of the key issues and controversies as evidenced in the literature specific to your topic.

Longitudinal research: a research design in which data from the same source or similar sources are collected in relation to a phenomenon over a period of time, typically at regular intervals.

Methodology: an overarching framework for your orientation and your procedures, signalling the philosophy underpinning what you plan to do in your research.

Methods: the approaches that you will take to gather your data and the approach you will take to analyze your data.

Mixed method research: research designs that combine both qualitative and quantitative research procedures; the data from the separate designs are integrated or mixed.

Narrative inquiry: research designs in which personal experiences are recorded systematically using both traditional and contemporary methods through the use of, for example, artefacts, video diaries, interviews, journals and letters.

Numerical data: numbers and measurements which are used to form conclusions.

Observational data: occurrences of events which are observed and from which conclusions can be drawn.

Observation schedule: a data tool that assists the researcher in recording an observation of an event and in recording the frequency of the event.

Paradigm: a worldview linked to a set of assumptions about knowledge and truth.

Participants: the people who are involved in the research that are being tested, observed, surveyed or interviewed for information.

Positivism: a paradigm for generating laws and using deductive logic and observations to confirm causal links between variables.

Primary research: data collected from surveys, interviews, documents, experiments or tests.

Purposive sampling: a sample from the population comprising participants who are relevant to the study.

Qualitative research: research designs based on interpretivism, involving explorations of cultures, people and individuals, and focusing on in-depth understanding of what is going on holistically, in an evolving and circular way.

Quantitative research: research designs based on positivism, involving facts, numbers and measurement, and focusing on convergences as well as variation within a specific dimension or variable across and within a given population and situation.

Questionnaire: a data collection method comprising a set of questions administered to participants, known as respondents.

Reliability: the extent to which your research findings can be replicated by others and over time with the same conclusions drawn.

Research journal: a record, usually in the form of a diary, in which the researcher notes and reflects upon decisions made in relation to the research. It may include personal reflections about any aspect of the research.

Research objective: what you are trying to find out or understand in your research, and typically written as 'to investigate…' or 'to compare…' and so forth.

Research questions: what you are trying to find answers to through your research activity; they set sharp boundaries around and guide a focused research investigation.

Rigour: the extent to which your research is organized systematically and meticulously.

Sample: a selection of people or other data sources from a section of a larger group or population which is the key interest of the researcher.

Secondary research: data collected from research that has already been undertaken or published.

Survey: a research design that involves a set of carefully constructed questions which respondents will answer.

Theory: an idea, explanations or a set of propositions that explain why things happen as they do.

Theoretical perspective: the philosophical stance that you take to frame your research and to inform the process.

Triangulation: an analytic process by which findings are corroborated by using evidence from two or more different data sources.

Validity: refers to the robustness of a research exploration, and determines whether what we are measuring is what we think we are measuring.

Index